HOME GUARD
MANUAL
1941

HOME GUARD MANUAL

1941

With an Introduction by Campbell McCutcheon

TEMPUS

First published 1941, this edition 2006

Tempus Publishing Limited
The Mill, Brimscombe Port,
Stroud, Gloucestershire, GL5 2QG
www.tempus-publishing.com

British Library Cataloguing in Publication Data.
A catalogue record for this book is available from the British Library.

ISBN 0 7524 3887 5

Typesetting and origination by Tempus Publishing Limited
Printed and bound in Great Britain

INTRODUCTION

It all started in 1933 when Adolf Hitler became Chancellor of Germany. From that day on, war was inevitable. As Hitler slowly nibbled away at Europe, annexing country after country, the rest of the world stood and watched, neither helping the invaded countries nor stopping the aggressive German expansion into Central Europe. The 1938 Munich Agreement only delayed the inevitable. The invasion of Poland, however, was the final straw for the Allies. Both British and French governments had signed non-aggression pacts with Poland, and both were duty bound to declare war against any aggressor. When Germany invaded Poland under the pretext of border incursions by the Poles, Britain and France stood side by side with Poland. Both declared war on Germany and her allies but, by 6 October, thanks mainly to a Russian invasion of eastern Poland, war in the east was over, Poland was over-run and Eastern Europe was split into German and Russian spheres of influence.

And so began a period known as the 'phoney war'. The Germans and French faced each other with Britain's Expeditionary Force supporting the French. Along the Maginot Line there were numerous small skirmishes, and the RAF dropped propaganda leaflets onto German cities, but there was little evidence of war. For the winter of 1939/40 all was quiet in Europe and the war raged at sea instead. It was all to change in April 1940, with the invasion of Norway and Denmark by Germany and the landing of an Allied force at Narvik, in an attempt to prevent traffic of Swedish iron ore to Germany.

On 10 May, the invasion of France, Belgium, the Netherlands and Luxembourg started. The phoney war had ended and a German Blitzkreig was about to overwhelm Europe. Winston Churchill became Prime Minister that day too. By the eleventh, Luxembourg had capitulated, the Netherlands and Belgium were to follow soon after. By the end of May, things were hotting up and it was realised by the British government that the position in Norway was untenable. Despite re-capturing Narvik from the Nazis, it was obvious that troops were needed elsewhere and they were evacuated.

Our story begins on Tuesday 14 May 1940, with a short broadcast made on BBC radio. Directly after the 9 p.m. news, the formation of the largest civilian army ever seen in Britain was announced. Anthony Eden, in his new role as War Minister, spoke to the nation.

I want to speak to you tonight about the form of warfare which the Germans have been employing so extensively against Holland and Belgium – namely the dropping of parachute troops behind the main defensive lines… In order to leave nothing to chance, and to supplement from sources as yet untapped the means of defence already arranged, we are going to ask you to help us in a manner which I know will be welcome to thousands of you. Since the war began the government have received countless inquiries from all over the kingdom from men of all ages who are for one reason or another not engaged in military service, and who wish to do something for the defence of their country. Well, now is your opportunity.

We want large numbers of such men in Great Britain, who are British subjects, between the ages of seventeen and sixty-five, to come forward and offer their services. The name of the new Force which is now to be raised will be the 'Local Defence Volunteers'. The name describes its duties in three words… This is… a part time job, so there will be no need for any volunteer to abandon his present occupation… When on duty you will form part of the armed forces. You will not be paid, but you will receive a uniform and will be armed.

Eden finished by informing anyone who was interested that, 'In order to volunteer, what you have to do is give in your name at your local police station; and then, as and when we want you, we will let you know.'

Even before the announcement was over, men were leaving their houses and making their way to their local police station to sign up. The Expeditionary Force was being pushed back through France and it was obvious that the British Isles were next to be invaded. Churchill had already realised that the country's forces were committed elsewhere and that the defence of Britain itself depended on the men left behind.

It was those first few weeks of the Local Defence Volunteers that were portrayed so comically in *Dad's Army*. With no weapons, no uniforms and no training the LDV was, perhaps, worthy of the jokes and the image that has been portrayed of it for the best part of seventy years, but within a few short months, the LDV had metamorphosed into a highly trained fighting force.

It was expected that the LDV would be composed eventually of about 175,000 men, but a quarter of a million signed up in the first twenty-four hours alone. By the end of June, with the fall of France a mere two weeks before, Britain stood alone and one and a half million volunteers swelled the ranks of the LDV, a force that now equalled in size that of the regular army. While many of the men were ex-soldiers, most were totally untrained and a whole raft of books were published to help them with army skills they would have to learn – everything from drill to tank-killing, from patrolling to signalling, from making booby traps to ambushing the enemy. This one, actually published for the New Zealand Home Guard, is based on the score of books and pamphlets published by the British War Office for the Home Guard, as the LDV became know in July 1940.

All through the summer of 1940, the Nazis made their plans to invade Britain. Hitler eyed Britain from Calais. Operation *Sealion* was to see a combination of air and sea attack, most likely along the south and east coasts, with their flat beaches and easy terrain. In ports such as Rotterdam, Antwerp, and all along the Channel coast harbours, over 2,000 barges were prepared, awaiting the call. Soldiers were readied for the invasion of Britain and in Britain itself, there stood, waiting, the regular army and one and a half million volunteers of the Home Guard. Now armed, albeit with American First World War rifles, and uniformed in poorly cut denim, the Home Guard was being trained in all aspects of warfare.

At its inception, the Home Guard really did use metal pikes, bayonets welded onto poles, table legs, antique guns, shotguns, and anything that came to hand. With German air attacks almost every night, men went out with enamel cooking pots on their heads, with badly fitting uniforms, or no uniform save an armband. With the help of training, and lots of it, and manuals such as this, the Home Guard soon became a veritable fighting force, ready to defend Britain against the Nazis.

Again, the *Dad's Army* image would lead us to believe that the Home Guard was full of bumbling bank managers, ancient ex-soldiers and simpletons. It could not have been further from the truth. By 1942, the Home Guard was an extremely proficient and well-trained professional army in its own right, manned by men unable to fight because of their occupations, all vital to the war effort. This part-time army still managed to make a huge difference by releasing regular soldiers to fight abroad, in India and Burma, North Africa, the Middle East and South East Asia alongside the Americans, Australians and New Zealanders. Home Guard men also manned anti-aircraft batteries and coastal defences, as well as arms and fuel dumps and helped greatly in the preparations for the invasion of Europe. Without them, D-Day would not have been possible as soon as it was.

For those members of the Home Guard who showed a special aptitude there was a secret guerrilla army, highly trained to cause maximum disruption to the invading Germans. Little is known about the Auxiliary Units, even today, but there were three battalions covering Scotland, Northern England and Southern England, and full of the cream of the Home Guard. These men, all hand-picked volunteers, laid down months of supplies of both arms and food, ready to go into hiding the day the invasion started. Their job was to slow the invasion down by blowing up arms and fuel dumps, bridges, railway lines and generally causing confusion to the invaders. Most knew that if invasion came, they would be on suicide missions. If caught, they were liable to die at the hands of the Nazis and if not, they were not expected to survive for more than a month or so while in action.

The other members of the Home Guard learned the art of hand to hand combat and how to use a variety of weapons – from pistols to sub-machine guns, hand grenades and gelignite to home-made bombs. Many also invented some rather crude and basic weapons and had access to flamethrowers, mortars and larger field guns. By mid-1944, it was obvious that the Home Guard was becoming unnecessary. At its peak, over 1,793,000 men were in the service and during the war 1,206 had died on duty. With Churchill's personal intervention the men of the Home Guard were allowed to keep their boots and battledress, scant recompense for the four years of almost-free service they had given to their country.

By the early 1960s, despite a brief resurrection in the 1950s due to the Cold War threat, the Home Guard had become just a memory for most men and women. But all this was to change when writer Jimmy Perry and director David Croft brought *Dad's Army* to the small screen in 1968, with some eighty episodes being made over ten series. It followed the story of Walmington-on-Sea's Home Guard troop from May 1940 until mid-1942 with the last episode being shown on 13 November 1977 – appropriately Remembrance Sunday.

Repeated constantly ever since, *Dad's Army* portrayed an image of bumbling leaders, incompetence and lack of weapons. For its first few months, this portrayal of the LDV and Home Guard is pretty accurate but within a short while nothing could have been further from the truth. The Home Guard had become a highly trained, efficient force, created at a moment of great danger and with ten times the expected number of willing recruits. What *Dad's Army* has done is to keep the spirit of the Home Guard alive.

FOREWORD

By Lt-Col Sir Thomas Moore, C.B.E., O.B.E., M.P.

I commend this little book with confidence to every member of the Home Guard. In these few pages is all the essential information which will enable us to perform our tasks with efficiency and success.

I am glad that the Prime Minister has indicated his desire that our name should be changed and that the Secretary of State for War has confirmed the alteration. As I conceive it our strategy in the remaining stages of this war is to sweep the sky clear of enemy planes, to destroy the Italian Fleet, to intensify our economic blockade, and then with freedom of choice to land once again our Expeditionary Force on the shores of the Continent to carry out its appointed and inevitable task of defeating the enemy in the field.

While that final event is taking place the Home Guard will become the defenders of these Islands and this handbook has in simple and homely phraseology indicated exactly how we should fit ourselves to discharge that duty.

I ask that every member of our great National Volunteer Army shall read and study this text book with the conviction that in doing so he will add to his capacity to achieve the job he has undertaken, that is, to defend our country if necessary to the last man.

Whether it be on the beaches, in the valleys, or through the streets, I am confident we shall succeed; and so free our country, Europe, the Empire and the World, from the terror, ignominy and despair which Nazi domination seeks to impose on its victims.

House of Commons,
29 July 1940.

CONTENTS.

CHAPTER I.—INTRODUCTION.

CHAPTER II.—DRILL.

CHAPTER III.—SMALL ARMS TRAINING I.: GENERAL.

CHAPTER IV.—SMALL ARMS TRAINING II.: THE RIFLE.

CHAPTER V.—SMALL ARMS TRAINING III.:
OTHER WEAPONS.

CHAPTER VI.—FIELDCRAFT.

CHAPTER VII.—MAPPING AND RECONNAISSANCE.

CHAPTER VIII.—FIELD ENGINEERING.

CHAPTER IX.—SIGNALLING AND MESSAGES.

CHAPTER X.—ELEMENTARY TACTICS.

CHAPTER XI.—TRANSPORT.

CHAPTER XII.—TRAINING.

APPENDICES.

CHAPTER I.

Introduction.

1—Objects of the Manual. 2—Role of the Home Guard.
3—Organization. 4—Outline of Training. 5—Drill and Discipline.
6—Co-ordination with the Army. 7—Co-ordination with Other
Organizations.

1—Objects of the Manual.

This Manual deals with the organization and training of
Home Guard units. It gives unit commanders enough details of
elementary training in those branches for which manuals are not
readily available to enable them to do effective work. It sets
out the details of the new drill when these differ from the drill of
twenty years ago, and so will help to get uniformity. A number
of minor changes have been made recently by the Army. These
have been incorporated, and the drill set out has the approval of
the Dominion Commander and so is to be considered the official
drill for the Home Guard. It gives working details for the hand-
ling of automatic weapons not available for training but possibly
available in the field, so that men untrained in the use of these
weapons can work them by referring to the manual.

2—Role of the Home Guard.

(A) The primary object of the Home Guard is to have available
an organized body of men trained to offer stout resistance
in every district, and to meet any military emergency until
trained troops can be brought up.

(B) Possible forms of enemy action against this country are, in
order of their probability:—

    (i.) Naval action against shipping and land objectives within
range of the coast.

    (ii.) Sabotage of the means of production and transport:
freezing works, roads and railways, hydro-electric plant,
etc.

(iii.) Raids by aircraft operating from aircraft-carriers.

(iv.) Small local landing parties with limited objectives as in (ii.)

(v.) Full-scale invasion.

(C) Enemy objectives in these actions would be:—

(i.) To isolate the country by a naval blockade, mine-fields, etc., to prevent the sending overseas of troops and foodstuffs.

(ii.) To destroy or hamper the production of food supplies for overseas use.

(iii.) To demoralize the country by attacks on towns, creating panic and internal disorganization. (Conditions in this case would resemble those following the Napier earthquake.)

(iv.) In the event of invasion, to get immediate command of aerodromes and petrol supplies.

(D) The functions of the Home Guard to meet these emergencies will be:—

(i.) To maintain in coastal areas patrols and observation posts to report enemy activity.

(ii.) To take measures to prevent landing parties gaining a foothold, and to delay the movement of troops that have landed.

(iii.) To maintain communications by signals and runners.

(iv.) To provide men with local knowledge to act as guides and runners for troops operating in their area.

(v.) To guard petrol supplies, and if these have to be abandoned, to render them useless.

(vi.) To supply guards for vital points (railways, power stations, petrol stores and pumps, etc.) and for internment camps.

(vii.) To maintain order and morale in their district.

(viii.) If called upon, to reinforce the organization of the Local Emergency Precautions Committee in carrying out rescue work, fire-fighting, first-aid, evacuation of refugees, maintenance of food supplies and public services.

3—Organization.

(A) The Home Guard has been organized by the National Service Department, and is, until war conditions obtain, controlled by this Department. The Dominion Headquarters consists of Dominion Commander and a small staff. The Dominion is divided into four **Districts**, each with its Commander and H.Q., and each district into **Areas**, again with their Commanders and H.Q. The areas are subdivided into battalions. Towns will have compact battalions, of four companies and a H.Q. company. Country battalions will consist of scattered units, either sections, platoons or companies, each with a Unit Commander, with an appointment suitable to the size of his unit.

(B) **Country Battalions.**

As the nature of the operations that the Home Guard is likely to be called on to carry out will involve the manning of isolated section or platoon posts, each unit of the country battalions should train one or two members at least for each of the various jobs of a H.Q. company. For organization purposes battalion H.Q. will establish a skeleton H.Q. company, and the officers of this company will be responsible for the organizing and training of their specialist personnel throughout the battalion. Similarly in these battalions, H.Q. should make provision for a staff of instructors, to ensure uniformity of training within the battalion.

(C) **Organization of Battalion, Company and Platoon.**

  (i.) **Battalion:**

  H.Q.:—Commander.
  Second in Command.
  Adjutant.
  Intelligence Officer.
  Intelligence Section (see p. 113).
  Instructional Staff.
  Regimental Sgt.-Major.
  Regimental Quartermaster-Sgt.
  Six Runners or Cyclists.
  Office Staff.

  H.Q. Company.
  Four Infantry Companies.

9

(ii.) **H.Q. Company:**

> H.Q.:—Commander.
>> Coy. Sgt.-Major.
>> Quartermaster-Sgt.
>> Orderly Room Sgt.
>> Three Runners.
>
> And five Platoons—
>> No. 1, Signals.
>> No. 2, Medical.
>> No. 3, Transport.
>> No. 4, Engineers, and Tank Hunting.
>> No. 5, Supplies.

(iii.) **Infantry Company:**

> H.Q. as for H.Q. Coy., with the addition of a Second in Command.
>
> And four Platoons.

(iv.) **Platoon:**

> H.Q.:—Commander.
>> Sergeant.
>> Two Runners.
>
> And three Sections.

(v.) **Section:**

> Commander (Corporal).
>
> And seven men, one of whom may be a L/Corporal.

(vi.) **H.Q. Coy. Platoons** (see Section B above):

> (a) **No. 1 Signals:** These signallers will be the specialists. They will equip themselves with flags and lamps, and any other means of communication available (land lines, shutters, etc.). During the "alert" phase they will, under the direction of the battalion Signals Officer, establish day and night communication with neighbouring units so that signal stations are suitably sited, and their positions known before the second phase begins. They will also reconnoitre the battalion's defence area and site suitable stations, so that communication in the field can be established immediately the third phase begins. The size of the platoon should be sufficient

to allow the Coy. Commander to allot two signal-lers per platoon, while maintaining battalion and company H.Q. stations.

(b) **No. 2 Medical:** The commander will organize one Regimental Aid Post for the battalion, and make provision for four stretcher-bearers per company. All the men should be trained in camp and bivouac sanitation (see Appendix 1), and take over these duties when conditions require them.

(c) **No. 3 Transport:** Transport must be earmarked for the battalion, including the various branches of the H.Q. company. Road controls must be trained. The requirements and training are set out in Chapter XI.

(d) **No. 4 Engineers:** Demolition of roads and bridges (on orders from Army), establishment of road-blocks and tank-traps, the construction of temporary bridges, and tank-hunting are the main jobs of this platoon (see Chapter VIII. and Appendix 2).

(e) **No. 5 Supplies:** This platoon will be required to organize so that on the mobilization of the Home Guard the forwarding of supplies, etc., can operate immediately. They should know what stocks are held locally and where to go for them. They must have a knowledge of the daily supplies necessary for a platoon, and how they are to be sent forward.

(D) **Equipment.**

It is the responsibility of each unit to equip itself as far as possible. A great deal can be made available locally, and this should be collected in a store at the unit H.Q.

(i.) Every man, on mobilization, should bring with him:—
A haversack, two blankets, a waterproof coat or sheet, a great-coat, knife, fork, spoon, plate, mug, change of underclothes and socks, a serviceable pair of boots, soap, towel, rations for at least 24 hours, and a bottle of water.

(ii.) Gear that can be collected and stored will include:—
Tools of all kinds, buckets, kerosene tins, rope, barbed and plain wire, pickets and standards, nails and staples,

tins with lids (cocoa, treacle, etc.), thin glass quart bottles and corks, casks, drums, rags, galvanized iron, etc.

(iii.) Supplies can also well be earmarked or accumulated and stored. A typical list will include:—Iron rations, biscuits, oatmeal, flour, tar, kerosene, petrol, black powder, gelignite, fuse, matches, detonators, pencils and pads, tea, coffee. condensed milk, etc.

4—Outline of Training.

(i.) Enough drill to enable the men to be handled in a disciplined manner for training purposes, and in the field.

(ii.) Enough weapon training for the able-bodied to make them effective with the rifle or with such automatic weapons as may be made available.

(iii.) Signalling: Every Guardsman is to be trained in semaphore; specialist sections in morse.

(iv.) Fieldcraft and elementary tactics.

(v.) Map-reading and reconnaissance.

(vi.) Field engineering (weapon pits, wiring, obstacles, etc.).

(vii.) First aid.

(viii.) Local measures, civil and military, to meet any national emergency.

The degree of training will vary with the physical capabilities of the men and their experience, and to meet local conditions or national urgency.

5—Drill and Discipline.

Modern conditions of war, and especially those under which the Home Guard would have to operate, do not require ceremonial precision; nor can minute-to-minute orders be given in the field to any unit larger than a section. The essential, then, is not parade-ground training, but field training. Enough drill for practical purposes can be taught in three or four hours. Drill, as the basis of discipline and esprit de corps, is replaced by the keenness that exists in a voluntary organization, and by keeping the men fully informed about the purpose of their training and their responsibility for individual initiative within a broad scheme. Obedience is to be intelligent rather than automatic. Whenever time permits general directions should be given to the whole unit, and questions invited, so that all understand what the objective is, and what means are proposed for attaining it. Minor details can then be left to section commanders, and even individuals, to be decided on the ground.

6—Co-ordination with the Army.

The following arrangements to ensure close co-operation between the Army and the Home Guard have been agreed upon between the Army and Home Guard Headquarters:—

(i.) **Liaison between Army and Home Guard Headquarters and Units:** Army officers have been instructed to act in close liaison with their corresponding opposite numbers in the Home Guard, viz.:—

(a) O's.C. Districts, with District Commanders of the Home Guard. (Note: Area Officer, Dunedin, with the Otago District Commander, Home Guard.)

(b) Area Officers with Area Commanders of the Home Guard.

(c) Company Commanders, National Military Reserve, and Independent Mounted Rifles Squadron with local Unit Commanders, Home Guard.

(ii.) **Tasks in which Home Guard Units will assist the Army:**

(a) To provide beach patrols on stretches of coast not covered by fortress troops or independent companies or squadrons.

(b) To oppose enemy landings, and hold on until the arrival of Army units.

(c) To obstruct by movable obstacles the advance of an enemy who has effected a landing.

(d) To assist in carrying out demolitions and constructing permanent obstacles, **but only under the direction of Army authorities.**

(e) To provide guards for such vital points as are handed over by the Army.

(f) To provide guards for internment camps.

(g) To prepare sketch maps of coastal areas not included in the Army mapping plan.

(iii.) **Training Facilities:**

(a) Army Headquarters has instructed its officers to render every assistance to Home Guard units, as regards drill halls and training equipment. These facilities will be available only when not required by the Army.

(b) Rifles and ammunition will be issued to units of the Home Guard as they become available.

(c) The Army will provide instructors and arrange courses of instruction for the Home Guard whenever possible. Several courses have already been held.

7—Co-ordination with Other Organizations.

The Emergency Precautions Scheme, in a military emergency, will be concerned, amongst other duties, with the evacuation of refugees from an invaded area. This must necessarily be subordinated to military requirements. Each area will work out the roads needed for troop movement, and the Emergency Precautions Scheme will then devise routes that will not impede military movements.

In a civil emergency, such as epidemic or earthquake, the Home Guard will be available as an organized body to reinforce the Emergency Precautions Scheme personnel, and to work under their direction.

CHAPTER II.

Drill.

1—Squad Drill. 2—Arms Drill. 3—Platoon Drill. 4—Company Drill.
5—Ceremonial. 6—Field Signals. 7 Field Drill.

NOTES.

I. Details of drill as set out in this chapter are kept as brief as possible. Where no detail is given it can be taken that there has been no change in the last twenty years.

II. Words of command are in heavy type.

III. Where a count is detailed, the men should count their moves aloud in the earlier stages of training until uniformity of timing is attained.

1—Squad Drill.

(i.) **SQUAD.**

On this precautionary word, when the squad is waiting to fall in, all talking will cease, smokes put out, dress and equipment adjusted, the men stand at ease. When the squad is standing easy there should be an obvious bracing up, and a definite lift of the head as they come to the stand-at-ease position.

(ii.) **SQUAD. FALL——IN.**

First man up halts two paces in front of instructor, and stands at ease. Second man comes up on left of No. 1, halts, turns head and eyes acto right, raises his right arm, hand clenched, and moves with short, sharp steps until he can just touch No. 1's shoulder. Then he turns head and eyes to the front, drops arm, and stands at ease. Each man in succession does likewise.

(iii.) **SQUAD. ATTEN—TION.**

Left foot raised two inches from ground, and brought down sharply (the effect being that of a light stamp) with heel against right heel, and toes at angle of 30 degrees.

(iv.) **SQUAD. STAND AT——EASE.**

The same kind of foot movement as for attention. Hands behind back, hanging to full extent, right hand in left palm.

15

(iv.) **SQUAD. RIGHT—DRESS.**

Right-hand man stands fast. Remainder turn heads and eyes to right, at the same time raising the right arm, with hand clenched, and pick up dressing with short, sharp paces.

(vi.) **SQUAD. EYES—FRONT.**

Head and eyes turned to front and arm lowered smartly.

(vii.) **SQUAD WILL ADVANCE. QUICK——MARCH.**

Step off with full pace (30 inches) with left foot, bringing right arm smartly forward, waist-high. On the march arms swing from the shoulder, with hands lightly clenched, thumbs to the front and pushed forwards and downwards, and arms straight. If the arm is swung backwards as far as possible a full swing will result.

(viii.) **SQUAD——HALT.**

The command is given as the right foot comes to the ground. The next pace with the left foot is taken, the right foot is brought up and the hands cut to the side. The count is ONE (on the left foot), TWO on the final movement.

(ix.) **RIGHT TURN, BY NUMBERS. ONE—TWO.**

On "ONE" turn on heel of right foot, and half of left, the left heel being pushed downwards to brace the left leg. On "TWO" the left foot is brought up to the right, being lifted from the ground, and brought sharply down. Arms to be kept by the side. Similarly for left turn.

(x.) **ABOUT TURN, BY NUMBERS. ONE—TWO.**

On "ONE" turn about on right heel and left toe, locking the thighs just above the knees to retain balance. On "TWO" complete the movement as for other turns.

(xi.) **RIGHT (LEFT, ABOUT)—TURN.**

All turns are counted "One stop two."

(xii.) **RIGHT (LEFT) IN—CLINE.**

As for turns.

(xiii.) **SQUAD. MARK—TIME.**

Knees lifted to the front, and heels kept vertically below knees, with toes pointed downwards. Hands still at the sides.

(xiv.) SQUAD. FOR—WARD.

Command given as left foot is being raised. The squad steps off with the next pace of the left foot, getting a full arm-swing with this pace. Count "Down" on right foot, "Out" on left.

(xv.) SQUAD——HALT.

When marking time, command given as left foot is being raised. Left foot finishes the pace, and right foot raised and brought forward smartly down. Count "One" on left foot, "Two" on right.

(xvi.) MOVE TO THE RIGHT. RIGHT—TURN.

Turning on the march. The command is given as the right foot comes to the ground. The left foot is placed across the right, so that the right toe comes into the left instep. The right foot then takes the first pace in the new direction. Count "Down" on the left foot, "Out" on the right.

(xvii.) MOVE TO THE LEFT. LEFT—TURN.

As for right turn, changing left for right throughout.

(xviii.) SQUAD WILL RETIRE. ABOUT——TURN.

The command is given as the left foot comes to the ground. A pace is taken with the right (called the "check pace"), the left foot is placed across the right as for the right turn, and arms are cut to the side. On the next pace with the right the foot is brought to the ground facing the new direction. On the next pace with the left the foot is placed heel to heel with the right facing the new direction, and the squad steps off with a full pace with the right. Count "Check" on the right, "One" on the left, "Two" on the right, "Three" on the left, "Right" on the full pace with the right.

(xix.) SQUAD. FALL—OUT.

Squad turns to the right, pauses for three beats, and moves off smartly. Count "One stop two, one two three four," moving off on four.

(xx.) SQUAD——DISMISS.

(Assuming an officer is on parade.) Squad turns to the right, salutes, pauses three beats, and then moves off. Count "One stop two" (for the turn), "One two three four" (up for the salute on "one," down on "four"), "one two three four" (for the pause, moving off on "four").

2—Arms Drill.

NOTE.—All movements are done first by numbers, e.g.,
SLOPE ARMS BY NUMBERS: ONE, TWO, THREE; then with the squad counting the time aloud. The practice is for all units to count aloud all rifle movements, without further command, until uniformity of timing is attained.

In counting, movements are made on **"ONE,"** and a pause for "TWO THREE." **"ONE"** should be accentuated, and a tendency to increase the rate of counting checked.

STAND EASY: The hand is slid up the rifle to the piling swivel.

SLOPE—ARMS, ORDER—ARMS, TRAIL—ARMS, PRESENT—ARMS are unchanged.

GROUND—ARMS: The rifle is grounded at right angles to the squad's front, with the back-sight in line with the toe, magazine outwards. Count "One two three, one." Down on the first "one," up on the second.

TAKE UP—ARMS: "One two three, one." Down on the first "one," up on the second.

TRAIL—ARMS from order. No count.

ORDER—ARMS from trail. No count.

FOR INSPECTION, PORT—ARMS.

(a) By numbers.

ONE: Throw the rifle with the right hand across the body, the muzzle crossing opposite the point of the left shoulder, catching it with the left hand behind the back-sight, and right hand coming to the small of the butt. Both elbows close to the body, left hand opposite the left breast, and rifle three inches away from the body.

TWO: Release the safety catch by pushing it forward with the right thumb.

THREE: Seize the knob of the bolt with the right thumb and forefinger.

FOUR: Open the bolt.

FIVE: Return right hand to the small of the butt, thumb pointing up the butt and below the cocking piece.

18

(b) Counting the time.

Movement "ONE" is counted "One two three." "TWO" is counted "One two three." "THREE" is counted "One two three." After a pause the right marker, who will have previously slightly raised his bolt lever, knocks it down, and the click is the signal for the opening of the bolts, the squad counting "two three" only. "FIVE" is counted "one" only.

EXAMINE—ARMS: (No count.) The rifle is brought to the "standing load" position, butt in the groin, the right thumb nail being placed in front of the bolt to reflect light up the barrel. At the same time a half-turn is made to the right and the left foot carried out to the left front.

EASE—SPRINGS (from "port" or "examine"):

(a) By numbers.

ONE: The bolt is worked backwards and forwards six times with the thumb and forefinger, being closed and the lever turned down on the sixth time.

TWO: The trigger is pressed.

THREE: The bolt-lever is tapped down with the second and third fingers.

FOUR: The safety catch is applied by being drawn back with the forefinger.

FIVE: The right hand is returned to the butt.

(b) Counting the time.

Movement "ONE" is counted "One two three four five six, two three." The bolt closed and opened on each count to five, finally closed and lever turned down on "six." Pause for "two three." "One" trigger is pressed, pause for "two three." "One" the lever is tapped down, "two" the safety catch applied, "three" pause. "One" hand to butt.

ORDER—ARMS (from "port" or "examine"): The movements detailed under "EASE SPRINGS" are gone through, the hand returned to the butt is counted "one two three." Right hand then carried to outer band, "one two three." The rifle brought to the second position of the order, fingers of left hand stiff and across nose-cap, "one two three." Left hand cut away, "one."

3—Platoon Drill.

(A) DRILL.

(i.) **IN THREE RANKS, FALL——IN.**

The front rank act as in squad drill; the other two ranks do not raise their right arms, but cover off the front rank. Interval between ranks, one pace. With arms, men fall in at the slope, and come to the order and stand at ease in succession from the right.

(ii.) **CHANGE DIRECTION RIGHT. RIGHT—WHEEL.**

When in column of threes or in line. Right-hand man of front three, or right-hand man of front rank, steps short and moves round the circumference of a circle of 4ft. radius until the three of the rank are in line in the new direction, when he resumes the normal pace.

(iii.) **FORWARD,** given during a wheel.

The platoon moves ahead in the direction they are facing when the command is given.

(iv.) **CHANGE DIRECTION RIGHT. RIGHT——FORM.**

(a) From the halt: The right-hand man of the front rank takes a full turn to the right, the remainder of the front rank a half turn, the other ranks stand fast. On the command "QUICK MARCH" the right-hand man takes two paces forward and marks time, the remainder of the platoon move into their corresponding places on his left, and mark time when in position.

(b) On the march, the right-hand man takes a full turn to the right, moves forward two paces, and marks time; the remainder act as in (a).

(c) If **"AT THE HALT"** precedes the words "RIGHT FORM" the men halt instead of marking time when they reach their positions.

(v.) **ON THE LEFT FORM—PLATOON** (platoon in column of route).

(a) From the halt, no movement until the command "QUICK MARCH." The left-hand man of the leading three takes two paces forward and marks time. The remainder move round to his left and take up their places in line facing the direction in which the column of route was facing, and mark time.

20

(b) On the march, the left-hand man of the leading three moves on two paces and marks time, the remainder moving as in (a).

(c) If **"AT THE HALT"** precedes the command, the men halt on reaching their positions.

(vi.) **OPEN ORDER—MARCH** (for inspection).

The front rank takes two paces forward, the rear rank two paces back. Count "one, one two."

(vii.) **CLOSE ORDER—MARCH.**

The ranks move back to one-pace interval, with the same count.

(viii.) **REAR RANKS UP—MOVE.**

Given when a demonstration is being given to a platoon, to enable the rear ranks to see. The ranks move up (at the short trail with arms) and fill in the gaps between the front rank men.

(ix.) **BACK TO YOUR PLACES—MOVE.**

The rear ranks move back to their positions.

(B) CAUTIONARY WORDS OF COMMAND.

All movements involving a change of direction are preceded by a cautionary word of command. The direction in which the platoon would be facing if the sections were in line, and No. I section were in front, is the platoon's front, and any movement or turn in that direction will be preceded by "PLATOON WILL ADVANCE," in the opposite direction by "PLATOON WILL RETIRE." Any movement to the right of this direction will be preceded by "PLATOON WILL MOVE TO THE RIGHT," and similarly to the left. It is thus possible to have to give the command, "PLATOON WILL MOVE TO THE LEFT, RIGHT—TURN," if the platoon has first of all been turned to face its rear. When a change of direction has been made by a wheel, a form, etc., it must be remembered that the direction of the platoon's front has been changed.

Examples.

(a) Platoon in line.

(i.) **PLATOON WILL ADVANCE, QUICK MARCH.**

(ii.) **PLATOON WILL MOVE TO THE RIGHT, RIGHT—TURN.**

(b) Platoon in column of route.

(i.) **PLATOON WILL RETIRE. RIGHT—TURN.**

(ii.) **PLATOON WILL MOVE TO THE LEFT. ABOUT—TURN.**

(C) POSITIONS OF SUPERNUMERARIES.

(a) Platoon in line. Platoon commander three paces in front of the centre man of the front rank, the sergeant two paces in rear of the centre man of the rear rank.

(b) Platoon in column of threes. Supernumeraries do not change their positions when the platoon is turned to the right.

(c) Platoon in column of route. Platoon commander moves to a position two paces in front of the middle file, the sergeant two paces in rear of the middle file.

4—Company Drill.

(A) COMPANY IN CLOSE COLUMN OF PLATOONS.

(Interval for ceremonial parades, 13 paces from front rank to front rank. For training parades, interval as required.)

(i.) MOVE TO THE RIGHT IN COLUMN OF ROUTE. COM-PANY, RIGHT——TURN.

Platoon commanders turn with the company and move to their positions two paces in front of the centre file. Sergeants turn to the left, and move to the rear of their platoons. No. 1 platoon commander gives the command, "No. 1 PLATOON, QUICK MARCH." No. 2 platoon commander gives a similar command, soon enough to bring his platoon in at the correct interval (six paces) behind No. 1, and he leads them slightly to the left so as to cover off the leading platoon. The other platoon commanders act similarly.

(ii.) ADVANCE IN COLUMN OF ROUTE FROM THE RIGHT. COMPANY, RIGHT——TURN.

As in (i.), except platoon commanders give the command, "No. 1 (etc.) PLATOON, LEFT WHEEL, QUICK—MARCH."

(iii.) ADVANCE IN COLUMN, AT —— PACES INTERVAL.

No. 1 platoon commander gives the command, "No. 1 PLATOON WILL ADVANCE, BY THE RIGHT, QUICK—MARCH." Similarly the other platoon commanders, when the platoon in front is at the stated interval.

(iv.) AT THE HALT FORM CLOSE COLUMN OF PLATOONS.

No. 1 platoon is halted by its commander, and the other platoons when they reach close column distance.

(B) COMPANY ADVANCING IN COLUMN.
(v.) CHANGE DIRECTION RIGHT.

No. I platoon commander gives the command, "No. I PLATOON, CHANGE DIRECTION RIGHT, RIGHT—FORM," and when the form is completed, "FOR—WARD." Similarly the other platoon commanders as their platoons come into line with the right flank of No. I.

(C) COMPANY IN COLUMN OF ROUTE.
(vi.) AT THE HALT FACING LEFT FORM CLOSE COLUMN OF PLATOONS.

No. I platoon commander gives the commands, "No. I PLATOON HALT. PLATOON WILL ADVANCE, LEFT—TURN." The other platoon commanders disengage their platoons immediately and lead them into position behind No. I. No. 2 platoon should make two full wheels (without commands) to ensure that the rear files are covering, before they are halted. The other platoon commanders should act similarly. The C.S.M. will step out the close column distances for the platoons, and it may be necessary for the platoons to step short to give him time. Platoon commanders disengage from their platoons when they come opposite the centre of the platoon in front of them. Platoon sergeants carry on to their positions in rear of their platoons when the platoons are halted.

(vii.) See also p. 228.

(D) POSITION OF SUPERNUMERARIES.

(a) Platoon commanders and sergeants, as in platoon drill.

(b) Company in close column.

Company commander six paces in front of the centre of the front rank of No. I platoon.

Company 2 i/c three paces to the right of No. 2 section of No. I platoon.

C.S.M. three paces to the right of No. 2 section of No. 2 platoon.

Q.M.S. three paces to the right of No. 2 section of No. 3 platoon.

(c) Company in column of route.

Company commander six paces, C.S.M. four paces in front of middle file of No. I platoon.

Company 2 i/c six paces, Q.S.M. four paces in rear of middle file of rear platoon.

5—Ceremonial.

SECTION I.

PROCEDURE FOR THE COMPANY FALL IN.

1. The company should be on the parade ground five minutes before the time laid down for parade.

C.S.M.: "COMPANY."

All smokes out, dress adjusted, and properly at ease. C.S.M. takes up a position facing the right flank of the company position and two paces from where the marker of No. 1 platoon will be.

C.S.M.: "MARKERS."

Markers march out, No. 1 marker halting facing C.S.M. two paces in front of him, and stands at ease. The remainder fall in on his left, not at arm's distance.

C.S.M.: "MARKERS ATTEN—TION." "NUMBER." "OUTWARDS —TURN."

No. 1 turns right, the remainder left.

"TO CLOSE COLUMN DISTANCE" or "TO (SEVEN, etc.) PACES INTERVAL." "QUICK—MARCH."

Markers march off counting their paces, e.g., at 7 paces interval: No. 2 goes 7 paces, No. 3 14, No. 4 21. They halt, turn about, taking their time from No. 4. C.S.M. covers them off.

C.S.M.: "MARKERS—STEADY."

Markers stand at ease.

C.S.M.: "ON PARADE."

2. Men come to attention, slope arms, and march on their respective markers, dress, order arms, and stand at ease in succession from the right.

3. Officers then march on to the parade ground to a position about fifteen yards in front of and facing the company.

C.S.M.: "FALL IN."

4. Markers come to attention, take one pace forward, C.S.M. moves from centre front to a position five paces in front of the leading marker, covers the markers, and returns to his position in front centre of company.

C.S.M.: "RIGHT DRESS."

5. Remainder of company comes to attention, take one pace

forward and dress. Platoon sergeants turn about and supervise dressing. When dressing is completed—

C.S.M.: "EYES FRONT."

6. Head and eyes are turned to the front and platoon sergeants turn to the front.

7. When the company commander appears, the C.S.M. hands over the parade (saluting twice) and takes position three paces on the right of the centre rank of No. 2 platoon.

COMPANY COMMANDER: "STAND AT EASE."

8. All ranks stand at ease.

"CALL THE ROLL."

9. Platoon commanders come to attention, salute, turn to right, and moving via the outer flank, join their platoons.

10. At the same time—

PLATOON SERGEANTS slope arms, turn about, and—
"PLATOON ATTENTION."
"OPEN ORDER MARCH."
"RIGHT DRESS."
"EYES FRONT."

11. Salute and hand over to the platoon commanders.

PLATOON COMMANDER.

12. Inspects appointments and clothing of platoon—
"FOR INSPECTION PORT ARMS."
"EXAMINE ARMS" (if required).

13. Arms will be inspected.

PLATOON COMMANDER: "PLATOON ATTEN—TION."
"CLOSE ORDER MARCH."
"STAND AT EASE."

NOTE.—The outer flank is that opposite to the pivot flank, i.e., that by which dressing has taken place.

6—Field Signals.

(A) SIGNALS WITH THE HAND.

NOTES.—(a) All hand signals are preceded by a short blast of the whistle.

(b) In field drill no action is carried out following a signal until the hand is cut to the side.

(i.) **DEPLOY:** Arm extended over the head and waved slowly from side to side, the hand coming as low as the hips on each side.

To signal "Deploy to a flank" the arm is extended in the direction of that flank before being lowered.

(ii.) **ADVANCE:** Arm swung from rear to front below the shoulder.

(iii.) **HALT:** Arm raised to full extent above the head, hand open.

(iv.) **RETIRE:** Arm circled above head.

(v.) **CHANGE DIRECTION RIGHT (LEFT):** Arm extended in line with shoulder, then a circular movement made; on completion body and arm point in the required direction.

(vi.) **RIGHT (LEFT) TURN (iNCLINE):** Body turned in required direction, and arm extended shoulder high, pointing in the required direction.

(vii.) **CLOSE:** Hand placed on top of the head, elbow square to right or left, according to which hand is used.

This signal means close on the centre. To close on a flank, the leader will point to the required flank before dropping his hand.

If, on the march, it is required to halt as well as close, the halt signal will be given before the hand is dropped.

(viii.) **QUICK TIME:** Hand raised in line with shoulder, elbow bent and close to the side.

(ix.) **DOUBLE:** Clenched hand moved up and down between shoulder and thigh.

(x.) **LIE DOWN:** Two or three slight movements with the open hand, palm downwards, toward the ground.

(xi.) **AS YOU WERE, WASH-OUT, BREAK OFF:** Arm extended downwards with the hand open, and waved across the body parallel with the ground.

(xii.) **LAST ORDER COMPLETED:** The salute, followed by the hand raised vertically above the head, hand open and fingers together.

(xiii.) **ENEMY AIRCRAFT IN SIGHT:** Both arms held above the head and the hands waved.

(B) SIGNALS WITH THE RIFLE.

(i.) **ENEMY IN SIGHT IN SMALL NUMBERS:** Rifle held above the head at the full extent of the arm, parallel with the ground, muzzle pointing to the front.

(ii.) **ENEMY IN SIGHT IN LARGE NUMBERS:** The rifle held as in previous signal, but raised and lowered frequently.

(iii.) **NO ENEMY IN SIGHT:** The rifle held up to the full extent of the arm, muzzle pointing up.

(C) SIGNALS WITH WHISTLE.

(i.) **CAUTIONARY BLAST** (a short blast): To call attention to a signal or order about to be given.

(ii.) **RALLY BLAST** (succession of short blasts): To denote "Close on the leader" when a signal cannot be seen. Men double towards the sound of the whistle.

(iii.) **ALARM BLAST** (succession of alternating long and short blasts): To turn out troops from camp or bivouac to fall in or to occupy previously arranged positions.

(iv.) **ENEMY AIRCRAFT IN SIGHT** (a succession of long blasts): On this signal troops either get ready to engage the aircraft, or open out and take cover, according to previous orders.

(v.) **AIRCRAFT ATTACK ENDED** (two long blasts repeated at intervals of five seconds).

7—Field Drill.

(A) GENERAL.

Field drill is intended to make the men familiar with the various deployed formations so that they can be adopted quickly as circumstances warrant.

The following sequence of deploying and closing movements are to be regarded as drills only.

The drills are carried out by words of command as given, or by hand signals (see Section 6 (A), p. 24).

On halting, the units stand at ease. On getting the signal or word to move they come to attention, and move off with rifles slung when in close order, at the trail when in open order.

For training purposes the following intervals will be maintained in deployed formation unless otherwise ordered:—

Between platoons	....	100 yards
Between sections	....	25 yards
Between men		4 paces

(B) SECTION DEPLOYING FROM SINGLE FILE. QUICK TIME.

(i.) **DEPLOY:** The arrowhead formation is adopted. The section commander continues to advance, No. 2 goes to the right, No. 3 to the left, and so on.

(ii.) **CLOSE:** Section commander continues to advance, stepping short until his section are back in file.

(C) SECTION DEPLOYING FROM ARROWHEAD. QUICK TIME.

(i.) **DEPLOY:** Section commander steps short until the section move up into line.

(ii.) **CLOSE:** Section falls back into arrowhead.

(D) PLATOON DEPLOYING FROM COLUMN OF ROUTE. QUICK TIME.

(i.) **DEPLOY:** No. 2 section continue to advance. No. 1 section is led to the left by its commander to a distance of 25yds., and then continues to advance. No. 3 similarly to the right. The sections will then be in an arrowhead formation.

(ii.) On a further deploy signal, the sections deploy into arrowhead, as in paragraph (B) above.

(iii.) On a third deploy signal, the sections deploy into line, as in paragraph (C) above.

iv.) **CLOSE:** On the first close signal the sections come back to arrowhead, on the second signal into file, and on the third they are led to their original positions on either side of No. 2 section, who will step short until they are in position.

(E) COMPANY DEPLOYING FROM COLUMN OF ROUTE.

(i.) A company of three platoons will act similarly to the platoon as detailed in paragraph (D), except that No. 1 platoon continues to advance, No. 2 is led by its commander 100 yards to the right, and No. 3 similarly to the left.

(ii.) On a series of deploy signals the platoons deploy from column to file, to arrowhead, to line, as above.

(iii.) On the succession of close signals the sections close to arrowhead, to file, to platoon in column of route, and finally the platoons to company in column of route.

(iv.) The platoons of a company of four platoons will deploy from column of route on a prearranged plan, e.g., diamond or square formation.

(F) When the men are familiar with these movements, they will carry them out at the double, coming to quick time when their positions are reached.

   At a later stage, the men will kneel on the right knee when halted in arrowhead or file, and lie down when halted in line.

(G) The men must then be exercised first in quick time, later at the double, in adopting the above formations to a given flank, and closing on a given flank.

   E.G.—A platoon deploying to the left from column of route. Quick time. No. 3 section continues to advance, stepping short until No. 1 and No. 2 reach their positions.

(H) It should be impressed on section commanders and men in the course of field drill exercises that the formation adopted in the field is at the discretion of the section commander, who must adapt his section formation to make the best use of cover, or to obtain the best fire effect. (See Chap. VI. Sect. 5c, p. 82.)

CHAPTER III.

Small Arms Training I.—General.

1—General. 2—Indication of Targets. 3—Judging Distance. 4—Fire Orders. 5—Anti-Aircraft Action.

(1) GENERAL.

(A) The fire unit is the section.

The unit of fire is one round.

Normal rate of fire: Five rounds per minute.

Rapid rate: As fast as a man can fire with accuracy. (Rapid range-practice is 10 rounds in 40 seconds.)

(B) All platoon and section commanders must study the ground in front of them from the point of view of fire effect. Having considered how the fire power of the platoon can be most usefully employed, the platoon commander allots FIRE TASKS to his various section commanders. These are known as FIRE DIRECTION orders. They are given in defence or in withdrawal, rather than in attack. In the absence of any fire direction, section commanders must use their own initiative.

(C) **Fire effect** depends on the following:—

(i.) Selection of fire position.

(ii.) Selection of target.

(iii.) Indication of target.

(iv.) Finding the range.

(v.) Whether to use concentrated or distributed fire.

(vi.) Clear fire-control orders.

(vii.) Good fire-discipline in the section.

(viii.) Due economy of ammunition.

(D) **Field of fire:—**

(i) The shorter the range the more accurate the fire, and the greatest value is obtained from fire combined with surprise.

(ii.) In attack long-range fire may call attention to otherwise unobserved movements. In defence, it may help the enemy. Its ineffectiveness will hearten him, and it will only serve to make him adopt more suitable formations, and to take better cover.

(iii.) Enfilade fire should be used whenever possible. This is particularly important for the light machine-gun, which can fire a number of bullets in a very short time along the same line of fire. It is especially effective when applied along a fence or other obstacle.

(iv.) In defence the extent of the field of fire must depend on the ground. A field of fire of 100 to 200 yards will generally be sufficient for forward posts if flanking fire from other sections or machine-guns is available, and if surprise can be obtained.

(v.) Steadiness and accuracy suffer if men are themselves under fire. Section posts should therefore be selected with an eye to cover from view and from fire.

(vi.) In attack, if the section is temporarily held up, the section commander must locate targets and engage them on his own initiative. In defence, he will be given his fire task, which will normally be to prevent the enemy crossing a certain area.

2—Indication of Targets.

A fire unit commander must be able to direct the fire of his unit at any target, however inconspicuous. An obvious target can often be described unmistakably by the direct method, e.g., "Enemy on bridge."

In slightly less obvious cases, the men should be given the direction in which to look: slightly, quarter, half, three-quarters, right or left, e.g., "Half-right—enemy crossing gap."

Some targets cannot be indicated without various aids.

(a) **Reference Points:** Prominent objects, about 20 degrees apart, within the probable target area, are chosen. They should be of different kinds, e.g., a tree, a house, a post. These objects should be pointed out, and the names by which they are to be known detailed, to the unit.

(b) **Division of Field of View:** In indicating these reference points directions may be enough, e.g., half-right, red-roofed house; or it may be necessary to indicate them by dividing the field of view into foreground, middle distance, and background, and these into right, centre, and left sectors. The reference point can then be referred to one of these nine divisions, e.g., "Centre background, single gorse bush."

(c) **Finger· Method:** Using one of the reference points, a less conspicuous target can be indicated by giving its distance in finger-breadths (arm fully extended from the shoulder) right or left of the reference point, e.g., "Red-roofed house, three fingers left, small bush on rise."

(d) **Clock-face Method:** This can be used as a further supplement to the above. It should only be used when there is a considerable command of view. The lowest part of the reference object is taken as the centre of a clock face, and directions are given in terms of the position of the hour numbers, e.g., "Windmill, right, four o'clock, two fingers, small rock."

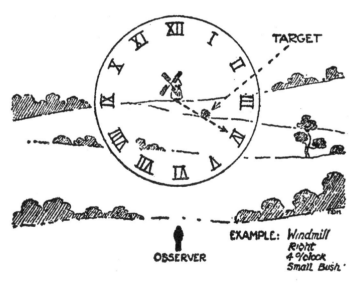

FIG. I—Reference point and vertical clock ray.

(e) **Training:** N.C.O.'s must be exercised in indicating targets, and their sections in recognising a target quickly when indicated on the standard scheme.

32

3—Judging Distance.

(A) Distances may be judged:—

    (a) By measuring the intervening ground in terms of some familiar unit such as a chain.

    (b) By objects of known size.

    (c) By bracketing, i.e., decide on the longest and the shortest distances the object can be, and take the average.

    (d) By halving, i.e., judge the distance to a point considered to be half-way, and double it.

    (e) By the use of key ranges and maps.

    (f) By the average of the estimates of several individuals.

All methods must be practised until it is found that distances can be estimated from the general impression, rather than by any one method.

It must be remembered that:—

(a) Objects are overestimated—

    When kneeling or lying.

    When both background and object are of a similar colour.

    On broken ground.

    When looking over a valley or undulating ground in dull or foggy weather.

(b) Objects are underestimated—

    When the sun is behind the observer.

    In bright light or clear atmosphere.

    When background and object are of different colours.

    When the intervening ground is level.

    When looking upwards or downwards.

    When the object is large.

Officers, N.C.O.'s and selected men will be taught to judge up to 1400 yards, others up to 800 yards.

Constant practice is necessary, under varying conditions.

(B) The appearance of men in various positions and at various distances are to be noted, under different conditions of light, background, etc.

Although no hard and fast rules can be given, normal-sighted men may make use of the following rules:—

    (i.) At 200 yards: All parts of the body are distinctly seen.

33

(ii.) At 300 yards: The outline of the face is slightly blurred. The buttons look like a stripe.

(iii.) At 400 yards: Outline of the body remains normal, but the face is not seen except under favourable circumstances.

(iv.) At 500 yards: The body begins to taper slightly from the shoulders. Movements of the limbs are no longer discernible.

(v.) At 600 yards: The head appears a mere dot; details are no longer distinguishable; tapering of the body very obvious.

(vi.) When the rifle is held in the aiming position the blade of the foresight covers a man standing at 400 yards, and a man kneeling at 250 yards.

(C) **Key Ranges:** Judging by the aid of some known or carefully estimated ranges shown on a range-card. To fill in a range-card:—

(i.) Mark off on the card the position from which the ranges are taken. Describe this position accurately.

(ii.) Select an unmistakable object in the arc or sector allotted for the section's fire task, and estimate its range carefully.

(iii.) Draw a heavy ray in the direction of this object, making its length as shown by the semi-circles correspond with its estimated range.

(iv.) Write a brief description of the object horizontally at the end of the ray, and the range as estimated.

(v.) Select objects to which ranges are to be recorded: these should include positions which the enemy may have to occupy, or near which he is likely to pass— obstacles, a gap in a hedge, etc.

(vi.) Keeping the card with the setting ray pointing in the direction of the object it represents, draw rays to show the directions of the points selected, making the rays of lengths corresponding to the ranges.

(vii.) Write short descriptions, in block letters, and ranges at end of each ray.

(viii.) Sign and date the card, and state how the ranges were obtained.

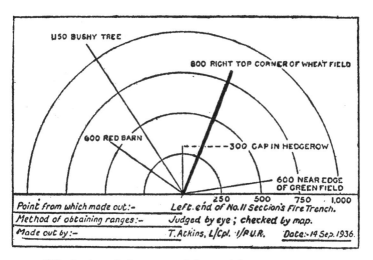

FIG. 2—A typical range-card for an infantry section-post.

(D) **Judging Lateral Distances:** All officers, N.C.O.'s and Scouts should know some measurement which will cover laterally one-tenth of a forward distance, i.e., one that covers 10 yards at a range of 100 yards, or 20 yards at 200 yards. With the rifle held in the aiming position the backsight protectors approximately do this.

4—Fire Orders.

(A) Fire control orders may be of three different kinds:—

> (i.) Normal.
>
> (ii.) Brief.
>
> (iii.) Anticipatory.

> (i.) **Normal:** A full and complete fire order contains the following, in the sequence given:—
>
>> (a) Designation of unit, e.g., "No. 2 Section."
>>
>> (b) Range, e.g., "Five hundred." (N.B.—Not five hundred yards.)
>>
>> (c) Indication of target. (See Section 1 above.)

(d) Number of rounds, e.g., "Five rounds."

(e) Kind of fire, e.g., "Fire" or "Rapid fire."

NOTES.—The initials D R I N K give the above sequence. The indication as given in the example is for concentrated fire. For distributed fire the limits between which fire is to be distributed will be named, but these will never be more than 3 degrees apart. (Three degrees is roughly measured by the distance apart of the knuckles of the first and second fingers, when the hand is held clenched at arm's length.)

An example of a distributed fire order is:—

"No. 2 Section—five hundred—from red house, right edge to point 3 degrees right—five rounds—rapid fire."

(ii.) **Brief:** Brief fire orders are used when the target is obvious, and there is no time for a full order, e.g., "Sights down, half right, rapid fire."

(iii.) **Anticipatory:** Anticipatory fire orders are used in both attack and defence, anticipating either the movements of our troops, or of the enemy, e.g.:—

(a) Attack: "No. 2 Section—five hundred—edge of wood half right. No. 3 Section is moving up on our right. We must cover their advance while they cross the open ground. Await my order to fire."

(b) Defence: "No. 3 Section—three hundred—quarter left—gap in hedge. The enemy are closing in toward that gap—when they are bunched I shall fire —fire on my order."

Or:—

"No. 2 Section—riflemen only— four hundred— hedge in front of farmhouse—fire when you see a target." (This is an example of a snapshooting fire order that might be given to a section in defence.)

5—Anti-Aircraft Action.

(A) When marching, magazines are to be charged with 10 rounds and sights set at 500 yards. No round is to be in the breech. The approach of aircraft is usually heralded by some warning like roaring of engine, but these heralds will be minimised by the 'plane taking advantage of sun, wind or clouds, and 'plane will as far as possible endeavour to surprise.

Speed of 'plane makes attacks short, but they will be repeated. If 'plane is attacking with gas it will fly low and will have to get into a definite position above target, and this will make it more vulnerable.

With long columns on the march the 'plane may not be heard, but alarm sounded by own troops firing. Attacks might be either individually by 'plane flying along a column or by several 'planes converging simultaneously from different directions. Former will give little or no warning, but with latter there will be some warning, as 'planes have to get in definite formation above target.

Discipline, training and morale play a very important part, and against undisciplined or demoralised troops air attacks may have a decisive effect. Enemy reconnaissance 'planes out to find troops must fly low. S.A. ammunition is of great value to prevent them achieving their object.

(B) **Principles of Small Arms Defence.** Main principles to be observed:—

(1) There must be a system whereby warning of the approach of hostile aircraft is conveyed to the troops.

(2) Maximum fire of all available small arms weapons will immediately be brought to bear on the attacking aircraft, provided that they are within range. It is only by adopting an offensive attitude that morale can be maintained and that low flying attacks by aircraft will be made so costly as to become unsound policy for the enemy.

(3) Subject to paragraph (2) above, units of all arms will present to the attacking aircraft the least favourable target according to the situation in which they find themselves.

(4) When movement is stopped it must be continued at the earliest moment.

(5) When troops are on the move, rifle fire will generally be quicker to produce and, therefore, more suitable than fire from the L.M.G.'s.

(6) In bivouacs, billets, or when otherwise halted, L.M.G.'s suitably tilted and concealed, should form the main S.A. defence.

(7) To be effective, fire must be controlled.

(8) Speed in opening fire is essential. This requires strict fire discipline training.

(9) Fire unit commanders must know beforehand whether they are to open fire on their own initiative or not.

(C) **Protection:** Every commander is responsible for the protection of his command against surprise and for concealing his dispositions from enemy ground troops and aircraft. Unless with small number of men, must necessarily march close together, and column must therefore be protected with L.M.G.'s picketing the area, or with M.T.'s moving within the column. It is essential that as great a volume of fire as possible be brought to bear, and if possible, L.M.G.'s. Normally all available rifles will be brought to bear.

When halted, L.M.G.'s should be posted in a series of triangles to protect the area, and in pairs at more likely lines of approach, but this depends on number of guns available. When troops are concealed, orders must be given when L.M.G.'s are to open fire, as it will betray position to enemy.

(D) **Warning and Air Sentries:** Quickness into action has direct bearing on effectiveness, both quickness of conveying warning and quickness in opening fire. The skill, steadiness and fire discipline of the troops then come in. Number of air sentries must depend on circumstances, but should not be less than two per company, and they must watch dangerous areas, especially into the sun. At the halt, should be on high ground. Duty is exhausting when properly carried out and must have constant reliefs.

(E) **Ranging:** Rifles and L.M.G.'s must be taken as effective up to 600 yards. Rough guide whether target in range or not:—

(a) At 600 yards aircraft is almost a silhouette; national markings may be visible, but colours will not.

(b) At closer ranges more details are visible.

(F) **Firing:** On command "Aircraft Action," adopt standing load position with muzzle of rifle as vertical as possible and load, leaving safety catch off; when firing, the safety angle is 25 degrees from ground. This is obtained when the forearm is parallel with the ground. This command may be "Aircraft Right" or "Aircraft Left." On command "Fire" always at rapid rate. Essential all movements quickly. Before new direction is given, command "Stop" will be given. With cross attacks, a lead of 12 degrees should be allowed in aiming. Aim in front, and swing rifle with 'plane and keep swinging when firing.

Measuring degrees is done as follows:—

First two knuckles of hand	3	degrees
Four knuckles, whole hand closed	8	,,
Four fingers extended	12	,,
Five fingers extended	19	,,

The only men who do not fire are platoon sergeant and section leaders. They retell the commands from the fire unit commanders. Fire control is by word of mouth where possible, and when attacked, centre of road should be avoided.

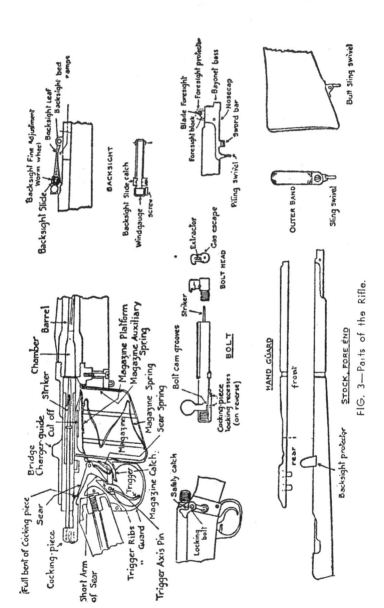

FIG. 3—Parts of the Rifle.

40

CHAPTER IV.

Small Arms Training: II.—The Rifle.

1—Parts of the Rifle.   2—Care and Mechanism.   3—Loading.
4—Aiming.   5—Firing.

1—Parts of the Rifle.

NOTE.—In elementary training the parts of the rifle are not taught apart from other lessons. As a part is named in lessons on care and mechanism, it is pointed out, and the squad is required to recognise it by name in future. The following list of parts is given for reference:—

Nosecap: Bayonet boss, sword bar, foresight, piling swivel, muzzle.

Foresight: Blade, block, protector.

Outer band, sling swivel.

Backsight: Slide, fine adjustment, worm wheel, bed ramps, lazy screw, protector, stud, rack.

Body: Knox form, chamber, charger guide, safety catch, resisting shoulder, recess, trigger, trigger-guard, trigger axis pin, magazine, ejector, sear, slots for bolt head retaining spring, gas vent.

Bolt: Head, extractor, gas escape, striker, rib, lever, knob, lug, cocking piece, full bent, half bent, long and short cam grooves, mainspring.

Magazine: Catch, spring, platform, auxiliary spring.

Butt: Small, trap, plate, heel, toe.

2—Care and Mechanism.

(A) **Recognition of Rifle:** A man should be able to recognise his rifle quickly. This can be done (a) by distinguishing marks such as colour of woodwork, marks and scratches, sling or sling lace, etc.; (b) by the number.

(B) **Cleaning:** Before cleaning the sling magazine and bolt should be removed and put in a clean place.

(i.) To remove the sling, unlace it at the lower sling swivel, and slide it out of the upper.

(ii.) To remove the magazine, release the magazine catch (behind the trigger, inside the trigger guard), and pull the magazine out.

(iii.) To remove the bolt, release the safety catch by pushing it forward with the thumb, raise the bolt lever, and pull the bolt back as far as it will go. Lift the head of the bolt with the knuckle of the forefinger to release the bolt head retaining spring, and pull the bolt out.

(iv.) Take the pull-through and oil bottle out of the butt trap; unroll the pull-through and run it through the fingers to make sure there are no knots.

(v.) Put a dry piece of flannelette, 4in. by 2in., in the middle loop of the pull-through (the upper loop, nearest the weight, is for gauze, if its use is ordered, the lower for armourer's use), wrap it round the cord and drop the weight into the barrel from the breech. There will be enough of the cord at the muzzle end to wrap round the hand once before the flannelette enters the chamber. Pull the flannelette through with one steady pull, taking care that the cord is not rubbing the side of the barrel. This is done until the flannelette comes through clean. Finish off with a slightly oiled piece 4in. by 1½in.

(vi.) To clean the other metal parts, use slightly oiled flannelette, with wooden matches or sticks wrapped in flannelette for getting into gas escapes, under the extractor, etc. The bolt head is not to be removed. Woodwork cleaned with oily rag. If the rifle is heavily vaselined, a preliminary cleaning with kerosene is advisable.

(vii.) After firing either ball or blank ammunition, six pints of boiling water should be poured through the barrel before pulling-through.

(viii.) The rifle should be cleaned daily, and again as soon as possible after firing.

(ix.) The oil bottle is put away first, the cap-end being put in first. Then the pull-through is held at the middle loop, given three turns round three fingers, the remain-

der is rolled round these turns, beginning at end
further from loop, and finally the weight is passed
through the loop. The weight is first inserted in its
slot by the hinge of the butt trap.

(x.) The magazine is replaced, small end first, and tapped
smartly so that the catch engages.

(xi.) Make sure, by comparing numbers, that the right bolt
is picked up. See that the head is screwed up, and
that the cocking piece is in line with the resisting lug.
Place the bolt in the body with the extractor uppermost and push it forward until the head is clear of
the resisting shoulder. Turn the bolt head over, and
pull the bolt back as far as it will go, and push the
head down until the retaining spring engages. Close
the breech, press the trigger, and apply the safety
catch.

(xii.) Before firing, remove all traces of oil from the barrel.

(xiii.) To examine the bore, hold the eye close to the muzzle
and look into the bore, not through it; gradually draw
the eye back, looking for rust, cuts and fouling. Look
from breech end to examine the chamber.

(C) Mechanism:

(i.) Guardsmen must know:—
   (a) How to remove bolt and magazine.
   (b) How to remove magazine platform.
   (c) How to replace these.
   (d) To see that bolt lever is in lowest position before
   applying the safety catch.
   (e) Half-cock, and how to re-cock.
   (f) How to load, and to charge the magazine.
   (g) How to unload by both ordinary and alternative
   methods.

(ii.) To remove magazine platform:—
   (a) Depress rear end of platform as far as possible, at
   the same time holding up the front end.
   (b) Pull the front end towards the rear end of the
   case until it passes under the front lips. The front
   end should then rise out of the case.
   (c) Tilt the rear end of the platform sideways, left side
   uppermost, and draw it forward out of the case.

(iii.) To replace the magazine platform:—

  (a) Insert the rear end of the platform in front of the rear lips, tilting it sideways so that the right side enters first.

  (b) Depress the rear end until the front end is below the front lips.

  (c) Press forward, guiding the front end through the internal ribs in the case.

(iv.) If the bolt lever is not turned fully down before the trigger is pressed, the stud on the cocking piece may strike full against the division between the grooves and prevent the striker going forward. If the bolt is then closed by hand the whole action becomes locked. The rifle is at half-cock, the trigger cannot be pressed nor the bolt rotated. The action is placed at full-cock again by drawing back the cocking piece.

3—Loading.

NOTE.—Before all drill and training involving the use of dummy, blank or ball ammunition, pouches, chargers and arms must be inspected.

(1) "STANDING—LOAD."

  (a) Turn half-right; carry the left foot to the left and slightly forward so that the body is balanced on both feet; bring the rifle to the right side, muzzle pointing upwards, butt against the front of the hip, grasping the stock with the left hand immediately in front of the magazine.

  (b) Release the safety catch, open the breech, take a charger between thumb and forefinger of the right hand and place it vertically in the charger guides. Then, placing the ball of the thumb immediately in front of the charger and hooking the fingers under the woodwork, force the cartridges down with a firm and continuous pressure until the top round has engaged in the magazine. Force the bolt sharply home, turning the knob well down, and with the forefinger apply the safety catch. Return right hand to the small of the butt, forefinger along outside of trigger guard.

Muzzle up

Turn half right

Eyes on the target

Finger along outside of trigger guard

Butt in front of R. hip

FIG. 4—Standing position: Load.

45

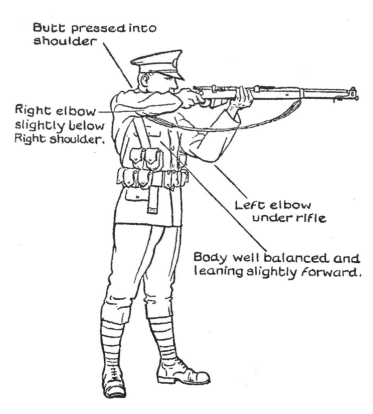

Butt pressed into
shoulder

Right elbow
slightly below
Right shoulder.

Left elbow
under rifle

Body well balanced and
leaning slightly forward.

FIG. 5—Standing position: Fire.

(c) To adjust the sights, hold the rifle in the loading position
so that the lines can be clearly seen. Press in the stud
on the side of the slide with the left thumb; move the
slide until the line is even with the graduation on the
leaf giving the distance named.

(d) If when the slide is returned to 200 it is found that the
line on the slide does not coincide with the graduation
on the leaf, press the stud with the left thumb until the
worm wheel can be easily revolved; turn the worm wheel
with the nail of the right thumb until the lines coincide.
The stud must not be pressed to such an extent that the
worm wheel entirely disengages from the rack.

(e) To come to the firing position, bring the rifle into·the
hollow of the right shoulder, press it in with the left
hand, grasp the small firmly with the thumb and three
fingers of the right hand, place the forefinger round the
lower part of the trigger, and take the first pressure. The
left elbow should be well under the rifle; the right elbow
a little lower than, and well to the front of, the right
shoulder. As the rifle comes to the shoulder, bring the
cheek down on the butt, keeping the face well back from
the right hand and the cocking piece.

(f) After firing, pause and bring the rifle back to the loading position and reload.

(g) Throughout the whole operation eyes are kept on the
target, except to glance down momentarily when placing
the clip·in the bridge charger guide.

(2) **TO CHARGE MAGAZINE,** proceed as for standing load, putting five or ten rounds, as ordered, into the magazine. Before
closing the bolt, the top cartridge is pressed down with the
thumb and the head of the bolt pulled forward with the little
finger until it has passed over the rim of the top cartridge.
Then the bolt is closed, the trigger pressed, and the safety
catch applied.

(3) **"UNLOAD":** As when loading, but after drawing back the
bolt, work the bolt rapidly backwards and forwards, without
turning the knob down until all the cartridges are removed
from the magazine and the chamber. Close the bolt, press
the trigger, and apply the safety catch. Lower the sights
and return to the order.

(4) **AN ALTERNATIVE METHOD OF UNLOADING:** To avoid
scattering the cartridges, remove the magazine and place it
in the belt; hold the left hand under the hole left by the
magazine and slowly draw back the bolt until the round from
the chamber falls into the left hand. Then close the bolt, press
the trigger, and apply the safety catch. Remove the rounds
from the magazine by hand, and replace the magazine.

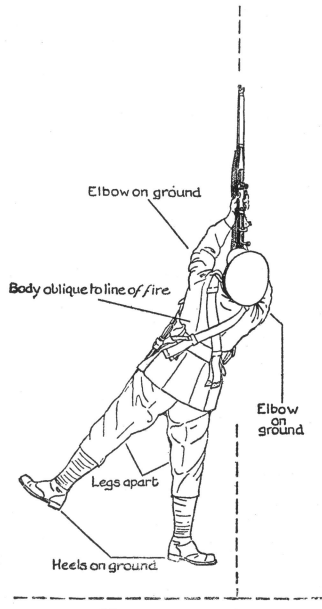

Elbow on ground

Body oblique to line of fire

Elbow on ground

Legs apart

Heels on ground

FIG. 6—Lying position (i).

48

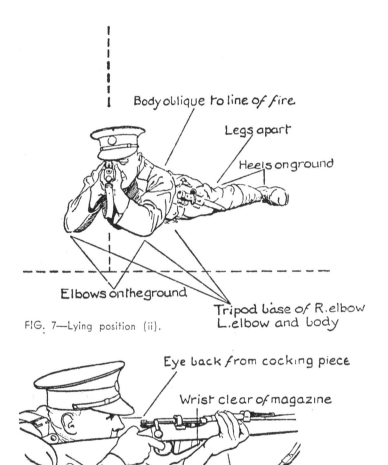

Body oblique to line of fire

Legs apart

Heels on ground

Elbows on the ground

Tripod base of R. elbow
L. elbow and body

FIG. 7—Lying position (ii).

Eye back from cocking piece

Wrist clear of magazine

Firm grip with both hands

Butt well into shoulder.

Elbows on the ground

FIG. 8—Lying position (iii).

49

Eye back from cocking piece

Wrist clear of magazine

Firm grip with both hands

Elbows on the ground

FIG. 9—Lying position (iv).

(5) THE LYING POSITION:

(a) To lie down, take a long pace forward to the right front with the left foot. At the same time change the rifle into the left hand, grasping it at the point of balance. Place the right hand on the ground in line with the left foot, and lie down; during this movement push the rifle forward in the direction of the target and lower it to the ground; the left arm will now be extended to the front. (See Fig. 6.)

(b) Load and unload as when standing.

(c) To adjust sights, take the right hand off the rifle and draw the rifle back with the left hand, pivoting the arm on the elbow. Adjust the sights with the left thumb, avoiding any unnecessary movement of the body, and resume the loading position.

(d) To get up from the lying position, draw up the left knee as close to the body and as far forward as possible without unduly raising the body; at the same time place the right hand on the ground below the right shoulder, and draw back the left hand, grasping the rifle. Press up into a kneeling position, bringing the right foot well in advance of the left knee, at the same time grasping the rifle with the right hand in front of the band. Rise up and return to the order, bringing the left foot up to the right.

(6) **THE KNEELING POSITION** is used when firing from continuous cover, such as a low wall or bank, or in long grass, etc.

    (a) To kneel, take a walking pace forward to the right front with the left foot, at the same time grasping the rifle in

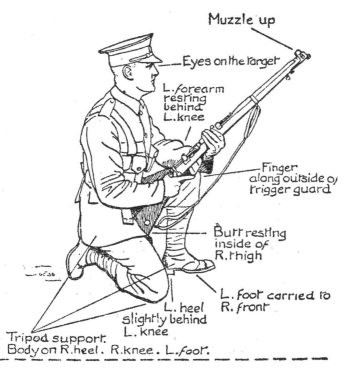

FIG. 10—Kneeling position: Load.

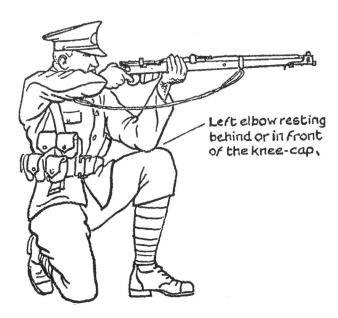

Left elbow resting behind or in front of the knee-cap.

FIG. II—Kneeling position: Fire.

the left hand as when standing, and kneel down on the right knee. If possible, sink the body on to the right heel, left forearm to rest on the left knee, butt of the rifle resting on the right thigh.

(b) To assume the firing position, the left knee will be in advance of the left heel, and the left elbow rested on or over the left knee; the left leg, hand and arm, and the right shoulder should be in the same vertical plane as seen from the front.

(c) Load, adjust the sights, aim, fire, and unload as in the standing position.

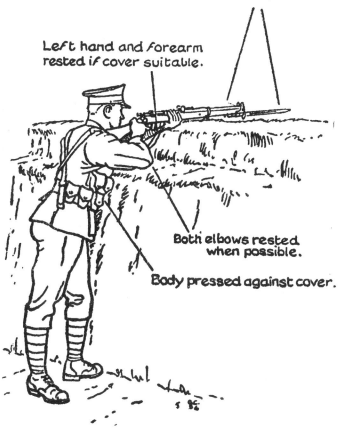

Bayonet and fore-end clear of cover if possible.

Left hand and forearm rested if cover suitable.

Both elbows rested when possible.

Body pressed against cover.

FIG. 12—Firing from behind cover. (i) Standing.

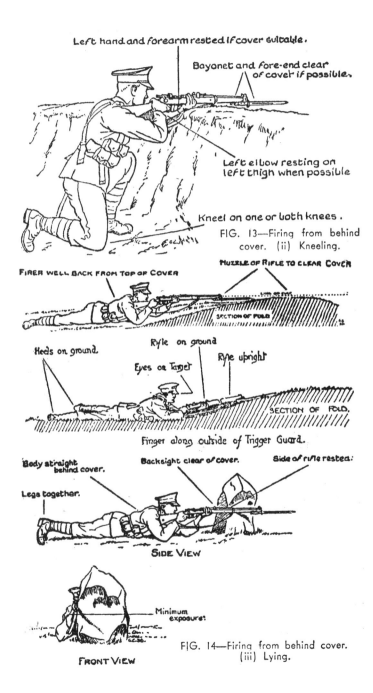

Left hand and forearm rested if cover suitable.

Bayonet and fore-end clear of cover if possible.

Left elbow resting on left thigh when possible

Kneel on one or both knees.

FIG. 13—Firing from behind cover. (ii) Kneeling.

FIRER WELL BACK FROM TOP OF COVER

MUZZLE OF RIFLE TO CLEAR COVER

LINE OF EYE

SECTION OF FOLD

Heels on ground.

Rifle on ground

Rifle upright

Eyes on Target

SECTION OF FOLD.

Finger along outside of Trigger Guard.

Body straight behind cover.

Backsight clear of cover.

Side of rifle rested.

Legs together.

SIDE VIEW

Minimum exposure.

FIG. 14—Firing from behind cover. (iii) Lying.

FRONT VIEW

4—Aiming.

(A) **A CORRECT AIM** is obtained by:—
  (i.) Having sights upright.
  (ii.) Closing disengaged (left) eye.
  (iii.) Look at the target, align the tip of the foresight on the lowest central visible portion of the target, the point of contact thus made being in the centre of and in line with the shoulders of the U of the backsight.

(B) **COMMON FAULTS:**
  (i.) Inclined sights.
  (ii.) Inaccurate centring of foresight.
  (iii.) Varying amount of foresight.
  (iv.) Focusing on sights instead of target.

(C) **AIMING OFF:**
  (i.) Aiming off for wind or movement is a man's own responsibility.
  (ii.) For wind, up to 400 yards aim off, for a man standing etc. still, one width; above 400 yards, two widths.
  (iii.) **For Movement:**
    (a) A man walking, one width.
    (b) A man running, two widths.
    (c) A man riding, or a vehicle moving, one width at all ranges.
       NOTE.—Rifle fire is seldom effective against a single man moving at over 300 yards, or against a vehicle at over 500 yards. Swing the rifle with the target, and continue the swing while pressing the trigger.
  (iv.) If aiming off in the same direction for both wind and movement, add the aiming off distances.
  (v.) If aiming off in opposite directions for wind and movement, subtract the aiming off distances.

(D) **NOTES ON AIMING INSTRUCTION:**
  (i.) With a tripod rest, or if this is not available, a couple of half-filled sandbags, on which the rifle can be laid steady, the instructor lays a correct aim. Each man in turn then looks at the aim as laid, being careful not to touch the rifle.

(ii.) Each man in turn then lays an aim and the instructor checks it. The squad can then criticise each others' aims.

(iii.) Any errors in aim will be pointed out, and their effect explained, e.g.:—
    (a) Sights inclined to the right will make the bullet strike low and to the right.
    (b) Too much foresight will make the bullet strike high.

(iv.) To test aiming and trigger-pressing, the instructor holds an aiming-disc to his eye six feet in front of the recruit and observes the sighting of the recruit's rifle while he aims and fires.

(v.) The disc is also used by the instructor to observe the quick aiming and firing required for snapshooting.

5—Firing.

(A) TRIGGER PRESSING:

(i.) Trigger has a double pull so two distinct pressures are necessary to fire a rifle. The first (3 to 4lbs.) is to be taken as the rifle is brought to the shoulder and aimed; the second (5 to 6lbs.) when the sights are aligned on the mark.

(ii.) The direction of the pressure is diagonally across the small of the butt.

(iii.) The first joint of the forefinger should be placed round the lower part of the trigger; the thumb and other fingers grasp the small of the butt, and the pressure is applied by a steady squeezing.

(iv.) In order not to disturb the aim, the breathing must be restrained when the trigger is being pressed.

(v.) The rifle must be kept firmly pressed into the hollow of the shoulder.

(vi.) During training for trigger pressing, the recruit should be aiming at a definite mark, and on releasing the spring he should say whether his aim was maintained. If not, he must state the direction in which the rifle was pointing at the moment of discharge, e.g., "Low right," "High," etc.

(B) RANGE DISCIPLINE:

(i.) Firing will not take place until the danger flags are hoisted. A red danger flag will be hoisted at the butts as a warning to cease firing, and will be kept up until the whole of the butt party is under cover. No one will leave the butts until the cessation of fire has been notified from the firing point. A red flag will be hoisted at the firing point when no firing is taking place. It will always be hoisted when the danger flag is flying at the butts.

(ii.) The platoon, etc., is divided into details, each of the number of targets available. The details are in line ten yards behind the firing point.

(iii.) A party from one of the waiting details is told off to fill chargers, to collect empty cases and chargers, to put ammunition on the firing points before the next detail moves up, to paste and replace targets after each detail has fired.

(iv.) The detail to fire first moves up to the firing point, is turned to the right, their arms inspected, and they are turned to the front. On the command "Load" they assume the lying position, and load their rifles, keeping the muzzles down and to their front and apply safety catches. Firing begins only on the command from the officer or N.C.O. in charge at the firing point.

(v.) When the practice is finished, the detail remains in the lying positions, rifles on the ground and breeches open, until the command "Unload" is given. They unload, and come to the position of "Stand at Ease."

(vi.) Arms are again inspected as in (iv.) above.

(vii.) On miniature ranges the party may move up to inspect their targets while they are assessed, grounding arms before they move up.

(viii.) On full ranges, values of groups, single shots in application, etc., are signalled from the butts.

(ix.) The detail which has fired moves back through the waiting parties, and takes its place in the rear. The remaining details move up one place.

CHAPTER V.

Small Arms Training III.—Other Weapons

1—General. 2—Bren Gun. 3—Lewis Gun. 4—Thompson Sub-Machine-Gun. 5—Webley Pistol. 6—Shotgun. 7—Service Grenades. 8—Home-made Grenades. 9—Molotov Cocktails. 10—Booby Traps.

1—General.

The first part of this chapter deals with several weapons that Guardsmen may be called upon to use and may first see under conditions where courses of instruction in the particular weapon are impossible. It is hoped that the brief description of each weapon will be sufficient to enable Guardsmen to load and fire the weapon should the occasion arise. It is stressed that these descriptions are very far from being complete courses in the weapons.

The second part of the chapter deals with home-made grenades. The large amount of commercial explosive normally present in the country makes these easily prepared and efficient weapons. A brief description is also given of the Molotov Cocktail.

2—Bren Gun.

(A) (i.) Fires .303-in. Mark VII. Service ammunition. Weight, 21lbs. Length 45ins. Can fire automatic or single rounds. Rate of fire 500 r.p.m. Magazine holds 30 rounds.

(ii.) **Change lever** is a small lever on the left of the body immediately above the trigger. There are three letters stamped above change lever, "A" forward, "S" centre, and "R" rear. When the change lever is at "A" the gun fires automatic; when at "R" the gun fires single rounds; when at "S" the gun is safe (safety catch).

(iii.) **Sights:** The gun has a foresight and a drum backsight which is fitted with an arm at the end of which is the Aperture. The drum is circular and grooved, and there

is a window in its rear face to enable range figures to
be seen. The scale is graduated from 200 to 2000yds.
On rotating, the drum clicks, each click giving an alteration of 50yds. in range.

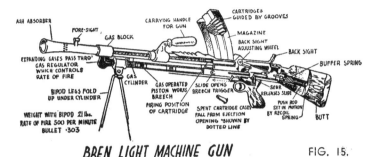

BREN LIGHT MACHINE GUN   FIG. 15.

(B)   (i.) **To strip gun** for cleaning purposes, etc.:

Remove magazine.

Cock gun and press trigger.

Push out body locking pin to right and slide butt back.

Draw cocking handle back, and push it forward again
{to draw piston to rear).

Hold return spring rod to the left, and draw out piston
and breech block.

Disengage barrel nut catch and rotate nut fully to the
right.

Turn carrying handle upwards and push forward. The
barrel will disengage from nut.

Push retainer pin level with opening in gas regulator,
turn it, remove regulator.

Hold backsight drum in one hand, and slide off butt,
etc.

Close magazine opening cover.

Press down barrel nut retainer plunger and remove
barrel nut.

Turn body upwards and remove bipod sleeve.

Replace in the reverse order.

(ii.) **To fill magazines:** Grasp magazine firmly in the left
hand, and press in the rounds with a downwards and
forward pressure. The magazine holds 30 rounds.

(iii.) **To load gun:**
Push magazine opening cover forward.
Place magazine on gun by placing front end in position in the magazine opening, then drawing the rear end of the magazine down.
Grasp cocking handle, turn back, and pull smartly to the rear.
Then push it forward, and fold forward.
The gun is loaded.

(C) (i.) **Immediate Action** (if the gun stops firing):
Pull back cocking handle.
Take off magazine.
Press trigger.
Put on magazine (fresh one if empty).
Cock gun.
Aim and fire.
   If after doing this, gun fires one or two rounds, then stops again:—
Pull back cocking handle.
Take off magazine.
Press trigger.
Cock gun by means of cocking handle.
Remove barrel and adjust gas regulator to next larger hole.
Replace barrel.
Put on magazine.
Aim and fire.

(ii.) **Stoppages:** If the gun will not fire after carrying out the above Immediate Action, the trouble is a jammed or empty round, or a separated case:
Cock gun.
Remove magazine.
Examine for any obstruction in body or chamber.
Remove obstruction.
Replace magazine.
Aim and fire.
   If there is no obstruction in body:
Put clearing plug into chamber.

60

Press trigger.
Cock gun.
Remove clearing plug and obstruction (separated case).
Replace magazine.
Aim and fire.

3—Lewis Gun.

(A) **Gun** is .303in. calibre, is air-cooled, and is operated by the action of gas and return spring. It is shoulder controlled and mounted on a bipod. Chief characteristic is ability to produce large volume of fire with employment of few men. Fires at rate of 600 r.p.m.. but as it is usually fired in bursts of five rounds, rapid rate of fire is 120 r.p.m. It is fed by a pan magazine holding 47 rounds. Gun can be used by right or left-handed firer. Weight 26lbs.

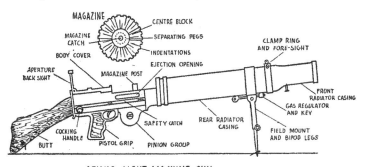

LEWIS LIGHT MACHINE GUN
FIG. 16.

(B) (i.) **Loading and Unloading:**

(a) Magazine: To load magazine, depress magazine catch, place rim of cartridge into indentation and nose between separating pegs, then rotate pan round centre block until round is gripped securely. To unload, reverse process.

(b) Gun: To load gun, place magazine on magazine post. and rotate clockwise until rotation ceases; then pull back cocking handle. To unload, remove

magazine, then with butt in shoulder, press trigger,
pull back cocking handle, and press trigger again.

(ii.) Holding, Aiming and Firing:

Gun is usually handled in lying position, firer lying in
direct line behind gun with left hand round small of
the butt, and right hand on pistol grip. Exert backways
and sideways pressure with both hands. The gun is fired
in bursts of five rounds, the firer pausing between each
burst to observe accuracy of last burst and to re-aim.
There is an aperture backsight, in the use of which the
first two rules are as for the rifle, the third being as
follows: "Align the tip of the foresight on the lowest
central portion of the target, the point of contact thus
made being in the centre of the aperture of the backsight."

(iii.) Cleaning:

(a) Before Firing: Dry barrel, bolt-head and piston
(gas affected parts) and oil working parts. Check
magazines, tension on return spring (13 to 15lbs.).
Tighten screws, check contents of holdall.

(b) During Firing: Clear gun. Oil working parts, check
tension on return spring, tighten any loose screws,
refill empty magazines.

(c) After Firing: Clear gun. Strip gun completely.
Pour five to six pints of boiling water through barrel,
then pass dry flannelette through until clean. Oil
barrel, Clean and oil all metal parts. Return spring
to 4lbs. pressure. Clean and oil all magazines.
Clean and oil barrel daily for four to five days
after firing.

(iv.) To Put Tension on Return Spring:

Remove butt, press trigger and pull back pistol-grip.
Holding pinion group hard against body of gun, pull
back cocking handle about one inch for each 3lbs. pressure required. Drop pinion, push forward cocking
handle, secure pinion in place by pushing forward pistol-
grip, replace butt. Test tension with spring balance on
the combination tool.

To Take Off Tension: Remove butt, withdraw pistol-grip, drop pinion group. With pinion down, draw back cocking handle one inch for each 3lbs. required taken off. Raise pinion, push forward pistol grip. Cocking handle will fly forward. Replace butt. Test tension.

(v.) **To Strip Gun:**

Cock action, then press trigger.

Remove butt (by depressing catch on under-side and rotating half-turn to left).

Remove pistol-grip (slide to rear).

Unhook pinion.

Remove piston and bolt by pulling back cocking handle and removing it. Then withdraw bolt and piston.

Remove body cover by grasping with both hands and pressing towards rear. (Note: At forward end of body cover are cartridge guide and two stop pawls.)

Remove Feed Arm (lying on top of body under body cover).

Remove body by removing body locking pin (where pinion and body join) and rotating anti-clockwise.

Reassemble in reverse order.

(C) (i.) **Immediate Action:** In teaching action when gun stops, action depends on position of cocking handle. If cocking handle is right forward, gun is in First Position. If cocking handle is anywhere behind this position, it is in the Second Position.

First Position: If gun stops in first position, feel for the cocking handle, and attempt to rotate magazine. If magazine rotates freely, change magazine. If it does not rotate, pull back cocking handle, aim and fire.

Second Position: If gun stops in second position, feel for cocking handle, pull it back, attempt to counter-rotate magazine, aim and fire.

If gun stops in any position, and there is no tension on cocking handle, change pinion group (broken return spring).

4—Thompson Sub-Machine-Gun.

(A) Fires a nickel automatic bullet .45in. Weight 10lbs. Length 39ins. Can fire automatic or single rounds. Rate of fire 900 r.p.m. Maximum range 600yds. Two types of magazines issued:—

(a) Box type holding 20 rounds.
(b) Drum type holding 50 rounds.

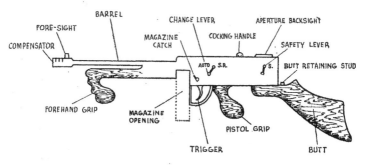

THOMPSON SUB-MACHINE GUN ·45-in

FIG. 17.

(B) (i.) **Change Lever:** By means of the change lever the gun may be made to fire automatic or single rounds. With the change lever in the forward position the gun fires automatic; with the lever in the rear position the gun fires single rounds.

If the moving parts of the gun are forward, and the change lever is at "Auto," it cannot be changed to "Single R."

Never ease moving parts forward until change lever is at "Auto."

(ii.) **Safety Catch:** The rear position is safety. The safety catch cannot be applied until the cocking handle is back.

Ease the working parts forward by holding the cocking handle with the right hand, pressing trigger and gently easing cocking handle forward.

(iii.) **Sights:** The gun has a foresight and three types of backsight:—
    (a) The cocking handle acts as a battle sight.
    (b) Aperture backsight up to 600yds.
    (c) Small V sight on aperture sight for use as battle sight.

(iv.) **Pistol Grip:** To remove pistol grip:—
    (a) With change lever in "Auto" position, cock the action.
    (b) Allow working parts to go forward.
    (c) Turn gun upside down, and press in pistol grip retaining plunger.
    (d) Press trigger and take off pistol grip.

(v.) **Cleaning Before Firing:**
    (a) Remove butt and pistol grip.
    (b) Clean barrel from muzzle end, making sure action is to the rear.
    (c) Take the brush, cover it with flannelette well oiled, and oil the breech.
    (d) Invert gun, and oil recoil spring, the two felt pads, and the face of the bolt.
    (e) Replace pistol grip (press trigger to slide it on).
    (f) Turn gun over and replace butt.
    (g) Press trigger, and allow working parts to move backwards and forwards several times to ensure even distribution of oil.

(vi.) **Cleaning After Firing:**
    (a) Remove fouling with flannelette.
    (b) Scour barrel with the wire brush (well oiled).
    (c) Dry barrel and re-oil.
    (d) Oil remainder of gun.

(vii.) **To Fill Magazine:**
    (a) **Box type** (20 rounds): Hold magazine in left hand with rib away from body. Press rounds into magazine with a downwards and backwards pressure.
    (b) **Drum type** (50 rounds): Undo winding key on front of drum. Undo small key on back of drum. Take lid off magazine. See that one of the rotors (arms) is opposite the opening in the magazine. Place magazine on ground and fill in an anti-clockwise direction. Replace lid, making sure the

stud on magazine is opposite opening in lid. Replace small key. Replace large key. Wind large key to **nine** clicks.

(C) (i.) **To Load Gun:**

    (a) With box type magazine—
Cock the gun.
Insert box type magazine, rib in groove.
Apply safety catch.

    (b) With drum type magazine—
Cock the gun.
Hold magazine with winding key away from body.
Insert magazine with ribs on magazine in grooves in body.

(ii.) **To Unload Gun:**

    (a) Box type—
Grip magazine with thumb on magazine catch.
Press magazine catch, and remove magazine.
Safety catch forward.
Hold cocking handle and press trigger, allowing action to travel forward. Repeat twice.

    (b) Drum type—
Grasp magazine with two fingers over and two fingers under magazine, and remove.
Safety catch forward.
Ease action forward as above, and repeat twice.

(iii.) In each gun chest there are three drum type magazines, and five box type magazines.

5—Webley Pistol.

(A) (i.) The .38 pistol is very similar to the .45 pistol, the only difference being that the Cam Lever Fixing Screw is on the left in the .45 and on the right in the .38. There is also the difference in calibre. Both are weapons for personal protection.

(ii.) The pistols are efficient up to 50 yards, although the extreme range is approximately 1800 yards. The bullet has great stopping power.

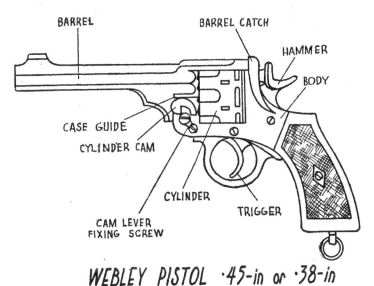

WEBLEY PISTOL ·45-in or ·38-in

FIG. 18.

(B) (i.) **To Remove Cylinder:**
Depress Barrel Catch with thumb, and break pistol.
Unscrew Cam-lever Fixing Screw.
Remove cylinder.

(ii.) **Cleaning Before Firing:** Remove all oil from exterior, bore and chambers.

(iii.) **Cleaning After Firing:**
Remove cylinder.
Remove superficial fouling.
Clean barrel till no more fouling comes away.
Oil bore and chambers.
Oil outside of pistol.
Replace cylinder.

(C) (i.) **Loading:**
Break the pistol.
Insert rounds in chambers, starting at 11 o'clock and continuing in an anti-clockwise direction.

(ii.) **Firing:** The pistol may be fired with either hand, or with both hands. It may be fired single action, i.e., cocking pistol each time by drawing back hammer with thumb of firing hand; or it may be fired double action, i.e., pressing trigger each time when pistol cocks itself. The pistol is fired by instinctive direction rather than by deliberate aiming.

6—Shotgun.

(A)　(i.) This is quite definitely a NEW ARM for the Home Guard. During the temporary shortage of rifles the shotgun will be an important part of our equipment.

For bridge guarding and for covering road-blocks it is probably equal and in some respects superior to the service rifle.

(ii.) The choke (left) barrel should have an ordinary cartridge, say No. 3 shot (No. 2 if procurable). The half-choke (right) barrel should have a specially prepared cartridge as set out in the notes below. Units are urged to demonstrate to all ranks the effectiveness of the shotgun as a defensive weapon.

(B) The results of actual experiments are set out below:—

(i.) Cartridge evenly ringed with knife. Supposed to allow the outer end to act in a somewhat similar manner to shrapnel. Very difficult to gauge correct depth of cut. Not satisfactory even with extreme care. Outer end of case sticks about half-way down the barrel three times out of five, causing delay before firing next shot.

(ii.) Cartridge cut straight through between centre wads leaving a narrow strip of uncut casing. Not satisfactory. In many cases very difficult to insert in breech: outer end sticks in barrel as above.

Don't waste time with either of the above methods.

(iii.) Extract shot from cartridge. Using as a mould the outer end of another cartridge case which has been cut in two, fill slowly with melted candle grease, dropping as much shot as possible into the grease as it fills. Allow to cool, and fill cavity caused by contraction until level. This slug, if allowed to cool until absolutely hard and then inserted in place of shot, is very effective. A few pellets break away and make a slight scatter round the main slug, which has good penetration.

(iv.) As above, but use candle grease only. A slug made in this manner will penetrate a 3/4-inch softwood board at 25 paces.

(v.) When time permits, the following is outstandingly successful:—Remove shot from cartridge. Take rounded end of broomstick 3/4in. in diameter. Sandpaper it down evenly until it will slide easily into the muzzle of your shotgun. Press it carefully into some firm sand (moulders' sand for preference). The sand should not be wet. Remove carefully. Melt shot from cartridge in iron frying pan or ladle and pour into mould. The resulting slug after cooling should be scraped lightly with a knife to get smoothness. Make sure that it will pass easily into the muzzle of your shotgun. Take the cartridge from which you took shot and pack the cavity tightly with slightly damp paper until there is just room to get the slug into the mouth of the shell, and lightly pinch end to hold in position. At 25 yards this slug goes through a sheep's carcase, and is a certain man-killer at 50 and even 75 yards.

(vi.) Moulding slugs in quantity, using bulk lead, can be done if care is taken only to insert the pattern to the correct distance in the sand, i.e., get the correct weight of lead in each slug. After 100 rounds no damage of any kind can be found in the gun, which is an old one. There is no excessive recoil.

(vii.) If bullet-moulds of correct size can be found, make round bullets; they have greater penetrating power.

7—Service Grenades.

There are two types of grenade:—
(a) No. 36 H.E. Grenade.
(b) Smoke Grenade.

No. 36 H.E. GRENADE (MILLS).

(A) (i.) Small grenade that can be thrown, or fired from a rifle fitted with a discharger. There is seven seconds between the release of the handle and the explosion (at present being reduced to five seconds).

(ii.) **Characteristics:**

Is a weapon for short range.

Comparatively heavy (can be thrown 25 to 35 yards).

Danger area about 20 yards. May wound up to 100 yards.

Dangerous on stony ground.

Thrower must be protected.

Useful in trenches, dugouts, street fighting, etc.

(iii.) **Description:** They arrive in boxes of 12 Grenades; 12 Ignitor Sets; 12 Gas Checks (base plates); 1 Base Plug Key.

Live grenades are black or brown in colour, with a red ring painted round the top about the filling screw.

Made of cast iron, deeply serrated. The explosive amatol or baratol. On unscrewing the base plug, two sleeves will be seen: one is striker, spring, etc., and the other for the detonator.

On top of the grenade are two shoulders to house the lever, which has a short and a long arm. The short arm is inserted into the neck of the striker. The lever is held by means of a safety pin.

(iv.) **The Ignitor Set** consists of:—

Detonator.

Five seconds of No. 11 Safety Fuse.

Cap chamber with a .22 rim fire cartridge with a gas escape hole covered with wax paper to prevent damp.

(B) (i.) **To Prime:** Remove Base Plug and place detonator in small and cap chamber in large sleeve. Replace Base Plug and tighten with Base Plug Key. The grenade is now ready for throwing.

(ii.) **Mechanism:** The Safety Pin is removed, taking care to hold the lever down by a firm hold on the grenade. When the grenade is thrown, the lever releases the striker, which is forced down and fires the .22 rim fire cartridge, thus igniting the 5sec. fuse. While the fuse is burning the gas escapes through the hole in the gas chamber, through the gas slot in the striker, up through the centre sleeve, and finally through hole in top of grenade. When fuse is burnt it ignites detonator, which detonates explosive.

(C) (i.) **To Throw:** To obtain direction, stand with left shoulder to target. Observe fall of grenade by jumping up.

(ii.) **To Fire:** The grenade may also be fired from a rifle fitted with a discharger. This discharger fits on the muzzle of the rifle, and has a shutter or gas port on the side, by opening or closing which the range may be varied.

> Closed—Range 200 yards.
> Opened—Range 80 yards.

> Every quarter the port is closed adds approximately 30 yards to the range.

(iii.) To fit discharger to rifle, unscrew the Base Screw, place recess over bayonet boss of rifle. Draw the claws down till they engage in top of nosecap, then tighten. Adjust gas port. Load with a Ballistite cartridge. Assume kneeling position with rifle inclined at an angle of 45 degrees pointing to the front, magazine uppermost. Insert grenade into discharger, and when well in remove safety pin. See that hands are clear of all metal parts. Pull the trigger.

(D) **SMOKE GRENADES.**

(i.) Smoke grenades are green in colour with a red band. When the lid (with the ring on top) is removed, there will be seen a Delayed Pellet (solder-like substance).

(ii.) **To Fire:** Remove lid, and place in discharger with the Delayed Pellet downwards (or with the word "top" to the top. On firing the ballistite cartridge the Delayed Pellet is ignited and burns for two seconds before firing the smoke composition.

(E) **BOMBING DRILL.** (See p. 228.)

8—Home-made Grenades.

This section deals with the preparation of grenades from readily available materials, and as this entails the use of explosives, some instructions will first be given on properties, safety precautions, etc. It is essential that all practice in this work be carried out under a competent instructor with permission of Area Commander.

(A) EXPLOSIVES.

(i.) Materials:

(a) The commercial explosive most used in this country is Polar Gelignite. This is a buff-coloured, cloudy jelly packed in 2oz. cartridges wrapped in waxed paper. These are packed in cardboard boxes containing 5lbs. Polar Gelignite becomes dangerous if exposed to the direct rays of the sun, or a hot temperature. It causes a headache if handled. If left in the damp for a long time it becomes greasy and mouldy, when it is more sensitive and dangerous. It is sensitive to a rifle bullet.

(b) A detonator is required to detonate gelignite. A detonator is a small metal tube about 1½ins. in length containing a small quantity of unstable, unsafe, high-velocity explosive. They must be **treated with great care**, as they are easily detonated, and the force of explosion is sufficient to blow off several fingers.

(c) Safety fuse of commerce is in 25ft. lengths, and burns at the rate of two feet per minute.

(ii.) Procedure: The sequence is fuse—detonator—gelignite.

(a) Lighting the fuse: Damp is likely to penetrate safety fuse, therefore cut off the first six inches. Cut the fuse slantwise. Place head of match on the slanting end of fuse and light by striking box against it. If in doubt, test the speed of burning.

(b) Fix the fuse to the detonator: Handle detonator very carefully, and do not drop or bend. To measure the depth to which the fuse must be inserted, take a piece of grass and carefully measure the depth of the opening in the detonator. Now measure this off on the fuse and mark with thumbnail. Insert square end of fuse into detonator carefully but firmly. Do not force or twist. Crimp with pliers well away from the explosive end of the detonator. The joint may be covered with insulating or adhesive tape. Carry wrapped in handkerchief.

(c) Insert detonator with fuse into gelignite: First make a hole in one end of the stick of gelignite

with a smooth pencil, etc., so that when the detonator is inserted no pressure is required. Carefully
insert detonator and tie in if necessary.

(iii.) **Safety Precautions:**

Do not smoke near explosives.

Do not use a knife on explosives.

Always keep detonators separate from other explosives.

(B) GRENADES.

There are three types of home-made grenades which are
very easily made, and which are effective. They are:—

(i.) Blast Offensive Grenade.

(ii.) Jam-tin Grenade.

(iii.) Pipe Grenade.

(i.) **Blast Offensive Grenade:** This is merely a stick of
gelignite with detonator and fuse. There are no flying
pieces of metal from the explosion, so the thrower does
not need to take cover, but can throw the grenade and
continue to advance. Its effect is due solely to the blast
of the explosion, and if one is thrown into a section
of men or into a machine-gun post the blast will at
least render the occupants incapable of putting up a
fight.

To prepare a blast offensive grenade, first cut a
length of safety fuse two or three inches (5 or 7½ secs.)
and crimp it into a detonator. Take one stick of gelignite, undo the paper at one end, and make a hole
with a pencil, etc. Before use insert the detonator and
fuse, and tie in securely by means of string, or better,
adhesive or insulating tape. Keep detonator and
explosive apart as long as possible (e.g., in carrying
up to a position).

(ii.) **Jam-tin Grenade:** This grenade throws numerous pieces
of metal in all directions, therefore the thrower must
be protected immediately after throwing (e.g., in a
ditch, trench, etc.). Depending on the size of the
grenade, they can be thrown 25 yards to 35 yards.

To prepare a Jam-tin grenade, take a small tin (jam
tin, malt tin, or any other tin of about 1lb. or 2lb.
capacity) and place in it a stick of gelignite in which
a hole has been made as above. Now pack nuts, nails,
bolts, stones, or any other similar material into the tin

73

around the central stick of explosive. When full replace the lid, in which a hole has been made through which the detonator may be inserted. Strap the lid on with a length of adhesive tape.

To throw, place detonator and fuse into the gelignite through the hole in the lid, secure them with a piece of adhesive tape to the tin. The grenade may then be lit and thrown.

This type of grenade may also be prepared with black powder in place of gelignite, in which case no detonator is required, merely the safety fuse directly into the black powder. This type of grenade is then very much safer than when prepared with gelignite.

(iii.) **Pipe Grenade:** This form was used in the Spanish War with good effect. The pieces of metal travel at a much higher velocity than is the case with the Jam-tin grenade, although there are fewer pieces of metal flying about after the explosion.

To prepare a Pipe Grenade, take a piece of heavy galvanised 1in. pipe as used for gas and water, cut off a piece about four inches in length, and make a number of criss-cross cuts in the side with a hacksaw. Into this place one stick of gelignite (which measures 4in. by $\frac{7}{8}$in.) and make a hole in the stick as before. Secure gelignite by making several turns with adhesive tape round the ends of the pipe. Insert the detonator and fuse into the stick of explosive, secure this by means of adhesive tape. To throw, light the fuse and throw.

(iv.) **General:** In practical work with grenades, the instructor must see that there is adequate cover for all. A ditch or bank about six feet deep with perpendicular sides is required.

A drawback to these grenades is the fact that they require to be lighted with a match, and in windy weather or rain this will be a very real drawback. A method of overcoming this is to cut short lengths of safety fuse, and dip one end in a match-head composition and allow to dry. Instead of lighting, it is then merely a matter of striking on some rough surface, e.g., a band of emery cloth round the left wrist. The preparation of such a composition should present little difficulty to one with a knowledge of chemistry.

Any of these grenades may be made more or less waterproof by tying a rubber sponge bag or some similar object round them.

9—Molotov Cocktail.

(i.) The Molotov Cocktail is an improvement devised by the Finns on the Petrol Bottle used in the Spanish War. It is a weapon for use against tanks, the method being to throw them from a ditch, etc., on to the tank. It is said that it takes five or six cocktails to effectively deal with one tank.

(ii.) To prepare these Cocktails, take equal parts of tar, kerosene and petrol. Mix the tar and kerosene, then add the petrol. This mixture is filled into bottles (quart beer bottles), a piece of cloth, etc., placed in the neck as a wick, and the cork inserted. To throw these, dip the wick in the mixture, light it, and throw it at the tank. The bottle breaks and the burning mixture spreads over and seeps into the tank.

(iii.) After the first bottle has been thrown, there is no need to light subsequent bottles; these are merely thrown on the tank. It is considered that the addition of sulphur to this Cocktail would be against the spirit of The Hague Convention and the Geneva Gas Protocol.

10—Booby Traps.

There are several devices for releasing a striker and so firing an explosive charge, when a door is opened, a box picked, etc. Ingenious engineers will be able to make up designs of their own.

An effective release for Booby Traps, either "trip" or "souvenir," can easily be made from an ordinary "breakback" rat trap.

Bore a hole through the wood just large enough to take the metal end of a 12-bore cartridge. Braze a bar, carrying a striker pin, across the backbreaker so that on release the striker hits the cap of the cartridge. A short piece of instantaneous fuse, a detonator and a charge of explosive complete the trap.

CHAPTER VI.

Fieldcraft.

1—General Instructions. 2—Cover from View. 3—Cover from Fire.
4—Camouflage. 5—Movement by Day. 6—Movement by Night.
7—Stalking. 8—Selection of Fire Positions.

1—General Instructions.

(A) The term **FIELDCRAFT** includes **initiative, cunning and intelligence** in the use of ground so that a soldier may arrive on his objective alive and fit to fight. The responsibility lies with platoon and section commanders to train themselves to put their training into practice in the field.

The experience of the men in a section will be so varied that nothing can be taken for granted; and nothing short of demonstration and actual experience will make the training of any value.

(B) (i.) Instructors must plan their course, and each lesson of it carefully, and rehearse their demonstrations. Not too much should be crammed into a single lesson, but as the men gain experience the exercises can be made more complicated and involve more points.

(ii.) After a demonstration or an exercise it should be freely discussed, and the discussion encouraged by pointed questions from the instructor. The points involved will be by this means more fully appreciated.

2—Cover from View.

(A) TYPES OF COVER,

(i.) **Undulating ground**, the least obvious and so the best. Considerable experience is necessary before its possibilities are fully appreciated. It can afford cover from fire as well, and gives no ranging marks for the enemy.

(ii.) **Hedges and bushes:** Good screens for movement, but give no protection from fire, and invite close attention from enemy observation posts.

(iii.) **Stream beds, ditches, road cuttings:** Excellent cover from view and from fire, but again they invite particular attention. If they are straight, they may be enfiladed.

(iv.) **Crops, long grass:** Good cover from view, but allow only a restricted field of view. Movement through them is often easy to see.

(v.) **Dead ground,** i.e., ground that the firer cannot see from his position, is to be looked for, and section commanders ·must be able to recognize what ground is likely to be dead to the enemy.

(B) Besides the types of cover listed above, it is possible to conceal one's presence by intelligent use of background:

(i.) Avoid skylines. Remember that the best observation posts, especially at night, are in low ground, and that the skyline to an observer may not be the crest of a hill, but at some point of the slope towards him. Whenever possible, go round obstacles, not over them: look round them, not over them.

(ii.) In bright sunshine shadow makes an effective background.

(iii.) Straight lines attract attention, as does movement. Irregularity will blend with the background: unnecessary movement will often give away a man's position that could have been concealed by "freezing."

(iv.) Avoid isolated bits of cover such as single bushes; these are obvious and will be watched by the enemy.

(v.) **Concealment is a matter of common sense and of good discipline.**

(C) **COVER FROM AIR.**

(i.) Observation from the air is more difficult than it appears. If the 'plane is high, the field of observation is very wide, and details are not easily picked up. Straight lines, movement, and objects that contrast with their background attract attention. If the 'plane is low, the speed makes close observing impossible. The essentials again are irregularity and stillness.

(ii.) Do not look up if a 'plane is passing over. The white-
ness of a face against the darker background may catch
an observer's eye.

(iii.) Broken light and shade, under the branches of trees,
will break up the outlines of men, guns, vehicles, etc.,
so that they escape detection.

(iv.) A body of men among trees or bushes, even if these
are not dense, are effectively screened from the air.

(v.) A newly beaten-down track through grass is sure to be
seen. Keep to already marked tracks whenever possible.

3—Cover from Fire.

(A) The following are the thicknesses of various materials required
to stop a .303 bullet:—

Shingle	9in.
Brick walls	21in.
Sand (in bags)	27in.
Sand (loose)	45in.
Earth	60in.
Clay	90in.

(B) **TYPES OF COVER.**

(i.) Road and railway cuttings. May become shell traps.
Can be improved by digging into the bank nearest the
enemy, to make good shelters.

(ii.) Walls and rock are good, but are apt to splinter, and
are easily ranged on. They do not as a rule give cover
from shells bursting behind them.

(iii.) Shell holes form ready-made weapon pits. A hole
should not be overcrowded. If a series of shell-holes are
occupied by a section, they should be connected up to
facilitate control.

(iv.) Buildings may be useful, but are apt to collapse under
shell fire.

(v.) Weapon pits are dealt with in Chapter VIII.

4—Camouflage.

Camouflage is the disguising of men, material, or positions when natural cover is inadequate or not available. If the background cannot be chosen to suit the thing to be concealed, then the thing must be artificially altered to suit the background.

It must be remembered that concealment does not end with the erection and occupation of cover. Carelessness in its use (movement, tracks, smoke, lights, ineffective fire) may give away a well concealed position.

(A) INDIVIDUAL CAMOUFLAGE.

(i.) Bright metal, light-coloured clothes (e.g., H.G. armlet), faces, hands, coloured puggarees will all catch the eye. These can be dealt with by smearing patchily with earth, discarding if possible armlets, puggarees, etc.

(ii.) Hard or straight lines stand out. These should be broken up, so that light and dark colours cross the hard outline. A strip of tape wound round the rifle, a few wisps of grass stuck in the puggaree, will effectively break the outline seen at thirty or forty yards.

(iii.) A twig fixed to the hat hanging above, but not covering the face, will in suitable light, throw patches of light and shade on the face and shoulders.

(iv.) In using grass, twigs of lupin, scrub, etc., care must be taken to see that it is changed when moving to a new position, if the vegetation changes.

(v.) Do too little with grass and twigs rather than too much. A moving bush invites a bullet.

(B) COLLECTIVE CONCEALMENT.

The concealing of a body of troops does not lend itself to camouflage. The chief object is to avoid being observed from the air; regularity of formation, unnecessary movement, shiny surfaces, smoke, anything that will catch the observer's eye, must be avoided. Overhead cover, trees, steep banks, shade are the requirements.

(C) CONCEALING POSITIONS. (See also p. 124.)

(i.) All weapon pits, gun positions, etc., should be camouflaged. Newly turned ground should be covered with fresh turf, left with enough soil to continue to grow.

The slope of the parapet and parados should be the same, so that there is no difference in the amount of light they reflect.

(ii.) If branches of trees, or bushes, are used to screen a position, they must be renewed regularly, for as they wither they stand out against the live foliage.

(iii.) Most important of all, strict track discipline must be enforced. Avoid the formation of tracks where they can be seen from the air. If this is not possible, work to a plan, and lay down dummy tracks leading past important points, to dummy but camouflaged positions. No short cuts which open new tracks should be allowed, and no man should walk beside a track and so widen it.

(iv.) Make sure that any camouflage work is done when the enemy cannot see you, i.e., during darkness. Otherwise your camouflage is a liability, not an asset.

(D) SOME "DO'S" AND "DON'T'S."

(i.) DO use your common sense to outwit the enemy.
DO avoid the skyline.
DO make use of natural cover.
DO avoid conspicuous landmarks.
DO keep in the shadow, and remember that shadow moves.
DO approach an occupied position under cover.
DO avoid all straight lines and regular spacing.
DO try to resemble your background.
DO garnish carefully by using vegetation, putting it in just as it is growing round about.
DO remember to renew dead vegetation.
DO keep turf or top soil when digging, to use on the parapet.
DO camouflage before daylight if digging at night.
DO take extra care when you are tired.

(ii.) DON'T be careless and give away your comrades.
DON'T look up at an aeroplane.
DON'T expose yourself needlessly.
DON'T move unless you have to, and then think how you can move under cover.
DON'T expose a white face or hands against a dark background. Rub them with earth.

DON'T use artificial camouflage if natural means of
concealment are available.

DON'T use vegetation unnaturally.

DON'T smooth down a parapet by patting it.

DON'T expose a position by making tracks to or
round it.

DON'T expose light or make a great deal of smoke.

DON'T stand with legs apart or with hands on hips.

5—Movement by Day.

(A) LINES OF ADVANCE.

(i.) The ideal line of advance provides concealment and
cover from fire throughout its length, and will offer
good fire positions and observation points en route.
Before any movement is begun the possible lines of
advance must be reconnoitred, and a decision reached
as to the most suitable.

(ii.) No line will meet all the requirements of the ideal,
and a choice will have to be made of the factors to
be sacrificed, depending on the particular situation,
e.g., a reconnoitring patrol is not concerned with fire
positions, but must have concealment and observation
points. A fighting patrol, once contact with the enemy
has been made and there is little further opportunity
for surprise, will sacrifice concealment for cover from
fire, and for the obtaining of a commanding position.

(iii.) When concealment must be sacrificed, open ground is
to be crossed as quickly as possible from one firing
position, with protection, to another, i.e., the advance
will be by bounds, from position to position. These
bounds will be covered by fire from other sections if
necessary.

(iv.) On reaching a new position the section commander
must look ahead and plan his next bound.

(v.) Crawling is seldom worth while except for very short
distances, such as the last few yards to a fire position,

or for conceaiing movement across a gap. For longer
distances it is tiring and causes delay. Success will
often depend on the speed of the advance.

(vi.) When crawling, the body should be supported on knees,
elbows and forearms. The head and the bottom should
be kept down. Knees must always be behind the bottom.

(vii.) It is possible to keep lower still over very short distances by lying full length and advancing either by
bringing one knee up alongside the body and pushing
forward, or by dragging the body, using only the
forearms.

(B) OBSTACLES.

(i.) Before crossing a gap the section commander must
consider what target the section will offer as it crosses.
If the gap is narrow it will pay to get the section
together and cross in a single rush. If it is wide, men
must be sent over in irregular groups at irregular
intervals. The first group or two can usually be of
three or four.

(ii.) If obstacles have to be crossed (e.g., fences, stop-
banks) much the same applies, with the additional point
that no two men or parties should cross it at the same
point.

(C) SECTION FORMATIONS.

(i.) The section commander has the choice of several
formations for his section: file, arrowhead, line, or any
irregular grouping. The formation adopted will depend
on:

(a) Control.
(b) Ground.
(c) Fire production.
(d) Enemy's fire.

(ii.) These four factors are conflicting, and a balance must
be struck to give the section the best advantage.

(iii.) The advantages and disadvantages of the regular formations are:—

Formation.	Advantage.	Disadvantage.
File:	Useful for certain types of cover such as hedges. Easy to control.	Not good for fire production and vulnerable.
Arrowhead:	Facilitates deployment to either flank, and gives a fair opportunity of fire production to the flanks.	Control more difficult than in file.
Extended line:	Useful for crossing ground under fire, and for fire production to the front.	Most difficult of all to control.

(iv.) A section commander should change the section's formation to meet the situation. He must be ready to manoeuvre within the section to make the best use of available cover.

(v.) When sections are deployed, commands will be replaced by signals, or by brief instructions, e.g., "Behind me in file," "Across the bridge and line the bank," etc.

(D) CONTROL.

(i.) The section commander must have control of all his section all the time. By day visual contact can be maintained over considerable distances. Scouts can be controlled, if necessary, by connecting files.

(ii.) Commands can be sent either by signals or verbally. The sections should be exercised in passing on verbal messages accurately.

6—Movement by Night.

(A) GENERAL.

(i.) Ground over which movement is to be made at night should be thoroughly reconnoitred beforehand by day, if possible. Aids for keeping direction should be noted, and plans made for avoiding or passing obstacles.

(ii.) Silence is of the first importance. Precautions must be taken to ensure that equipment does not rattle. Orders should be given just loud enough to be heard. Men should break step.

(iii.) On a still night noise carries far, and special precautions must be taken. On a stormy or windy night, natural noises can be used to cover noise of movement.

(iv.) On soft ground it is usually better to place the feet on the ground, heel first; on hard ground, toe first.

(v.) If a flare goes up men should fall flat and lie still before it ignites; if caught unexpectedly, they should "freeze," and only fall flat if the enemy open fire. Never look at a flare: it will be impossible to see in the dark for some minutes afterwards.

(vi.) If wire is encountered men should be taught to crouch low so that the wire can be seen in detail against the sky. If no wire-cutters are available the easiest way is to go through underneath, moving on the back and holding the strands clear of the body.

(vii.) If wire-cutters are available, the lowest strands should be cut and crawling resorted to. To cut wire, two men should work together, one holding the wire close to each side of the cutters, while the other one cuts. This method muffles the sound and prevents the cut ends flying back. A man working alone should hold the wire near a post, and cut it between his hand and the post.

(B) **KEEPING DIRECTION.**

(i.) General direction can be kept for short periods by the stars or by the moon.

(ii.) The prismatic compass can be used to find magnetic north at night, by the luminous arrow and patches. It can also be set to give a previously set bearing. Considerable practice is needed to make the use of a compass at night effective.

(iii.) Landmarks that can be seen against the sky will help to fix positions.

(iv.) If the route can be closely reconnoitred in daylight, members of the reconnaissance patrol can be used as guides. All men should be exercised in memorizing details of a route, and in guiding sections along such a route.

(v.) Roads, tracks, direction of the slope of the ground and direction of the wind will be additional helps.

(vi.). The section commander should move by bounds with frequent pauses (but not long halts) to check his direction by every means at his disposal.

(vii.) Routes at difficult points may be marked by tying white rag to bushes or posts; but care must be taken not to put these where they can be seen by an enemy patrol coming from the opposite direction.

(viii.) To ensure that large bodies of troops do not miss their direction, reconnoitring patrols can lay down lines of advance by means of white tape.

(ix.) Distance as well as direction must be checked. One man, preferably an officer or N.C.O., should be detailed for this job, and have nothing else to do.

(C) **CONTROL.**

(i.) Control at night is difficult. Sections must keep well closed up, and the bounds must be short.

(ii.) Visual contact should always be maintained. On very dark nights men can keep touch when closed up by holding the shoulder of the man in front, or, when crawling, by placing a hand on his ankle.

(iii.) After crossing obstacles, the leading man should kneel down and wait until the section is closed up again before continuing to advance.

(iv.) Loss of touch means loss of morale. It should be a rule that a message is passed forward the moment men behind are not closed up.

7—Stalking.

(A) Stalking is a series of exercises for individuals and for sections in fieldcraft. Each exercise should be designed to bring out points taught in previous lessons.

(B) The sequence of a lesson should be:—

(i.) **P**reparation.

(ii.) **E**xplanation.

(iii.) **D**emonstration.

(iv.) Interrogation.

(v.) Execution.

(vi.) Repetition.

Note the initials **PEDIER** as a key to work to.

(C) Exercises to cover the points of fieldcraft outlined above must be left to unit commanders to devise, taking into consideration local conditions. Exercises can well be repeated on the same ground under different conditions of light or weather.

(D) The following is a typical exercise. Others can easily be devised.

INDIVIDUAL STALK: Object, to practise men in the use of and cover when advancing.

(i.) **Preparation:** The ground on which the exercise is to take place must be carefuly examined by the instructor. He should decide all the details of his demonstration with reference to the ground.

(ii.) **Explanation:** The instructor explains to the squad that at a point which he indicates, 200 to 600 yards ahead, an enemy sentry group is said to be located. The stalker's task is to approach near enough to the post to be able to shoot with the certainty of killing.

The instructor will remind the squad that they must consider the following:—

(a) Final position from which to shoot.

(b) The best route to it, bearing in mind their previous lessons in fieldcraft.

The area to which the stalk must be confined will be indicated.

(iii.) **Demonstration:** In this exercise little demonstration is necessary. It is in the earlier training that demonstration must always be used.

(iv.) **Interrogation:** The squad are given a few minutes in which to study the ground, and individuals are then questioned by the instructor on what positions they have chosen as their objectives, and what routes they propose to follow. He will criticize their decisions where necessary.

(v.) **Execution:**

(a) The exact position of the post will be marked with a flag, and those of the squad not carrying out the stalk will move to the position and watch the movements of the stalkers. The stalkers will move up one at a time.

(b) One man will be told off as an observer. He will raise a flag whenever he sees a stalker, and keep it up as long as the stalker is visible. As he represents the sentry who is being stalked, he should lie at the base of the flag marking the post, and no one should draw his attention to a stalker.

(c) A second man will be told off as timekeeper; he will record the time taken for the stalk, and also the number of times the observer sees the stalker, and the duration of each exposure.

(d) The exercise for each individual ends when he fires at the sentry.

(vi.) **Repetition:** When three or four men have made their stalk the instructor will lead a discussion by the squad by calling attention to the good and bad points of each man's stalk under the following heads:—

(a) Did stalker select the best position?
(b) Did he choose the position first, and then plan his route?
(c) Did the selected route offer the best cover?
(d) Was the route chosen good from the point of view of "going"?
(e) Did the stalker have to crawl?
(f) Did he cross gaps successfully?
(g) When he stopped, did he remain motionless?
(h) Did he use any incident that might distract the observer's attention to cover his movement?
(i) Did he regulate his pace well?
(j) Did he succeed in his object?

A second detail of three or four men are then sent back to carry out the same exercise, with the benefit of the discussion to work on. Their stalks are similarly discussed, and the exercise repeated until each man has carried out a stalk.

The following is a suitable form in which to record events:—

Name of Guardsman stalking...

Time of Start.............................   Time of Finish............................

Distance of final position from enemy, in yards...............................

87

I	2	3	4
Exposures when advancing	Distance from post in yards	Duration of exposure in secs.	REMARKS (Nature and cause of exposure, etc.)

In Col. I enter 1st, 2nd, 3rd, etc.

Cols. 2 and 3 will give data for deciding whether the stalker became a casualty or not.

Col. 4 will help instructor to explain to the stalker and the squad exactly what mistakes were made.

8—Selection of Fire Positions.

(A) The characteristics of a good fire position are:—

    (i.) A good view of the ground or target to be covered by fire.

    (ii.) Cover from ground and air observation, and protection from fire.

    (iii.) Room for the free use of weapons.

    (iv.) Covered approaches.

(B)   (i.) Not all these will as a rule be available together, and the section commander must decide which will be sacrificed in any set of circumstances.

    (ii.) Isolated patches of cover, while giving cover from view, are usually to be avoided, since they give the enemy a good ranging mark and target.

    (iii.) A well-sited position in gently undulating ground will often meet all the requirements save cover from air observation. It will be harder to pick up than the above example.

    (iv.) A further consideration for a final fire position, before an assault, is that the ground between the position and the enemy is not so difficult or steep as to make the final rush slow, and so dangerous.

N.B.—See also Chapter X., Section 5B, p. 177.

CHAPTER VII.

Mapping and Reconnaissance.

1—Maps Available. 2—Reading and Use of Maps. 3—Prismatic Compass. 4—Plane Table. 5—Field Sketches. 6—Enlarging. 7—Reconnaissance Reports. 8—Intelligence.

1—Maps Available.

(A) The following types of maps are available at or through any office of the Lands and Survey Department:—

(i.) **N.Z. SERIES:** Four miles to the inch (1/253,440), five shillings per sheet. These maps show roads, rivers, railways, towns, and some spot heights. They are not contoured.

(ii.) **CADASTRAL SERIES:** Survey District Sheets, one mile to the inch (1/63,360), half-a-crown per sheet. As these maps are primarily produced for title and valuation purposes, property boundaries are the main features. They are kept up to date by constant revision.

The large **COUNTY MAPS** are produced by joining up the districts forming the county, and reprinting them. Roads, railways, rivers, etc., are shown, but a point to be watched is the number of "paper" roads (unavoidable in maps of this type) that are shown.

They are not contoured.

(iii.) **CADASTRAL SERIES** "40-Chain" Maps, half-mile to the inch (1/36,680), four shillings and sixpence each. These reproduce the data contained on the one mile S.D. Sheets (ii. above).

(iv.) **TRIG SHEETS:** Five shillings each. Maps showing the major trigonometrical survey stations only; bearings and distances of the main stations are given. They are useful for demonstrating the intervisibility of these points.

(v.) **TOPOGRAPHICAL SERIES:** One mile to the inch (1/63,360), five shillings each. Only one sheet (No. 134) is at present available. It shows all the detail that can be expected in an inch map. Contoured (V.I. 100ft.)

(B) **ADMIRALTY CHARTS:** Four shillings and sixpence each. These give the coastline, and off-shore soundings; but inland details given are quite unreliable.

Available from Mercantile Marine Office, Wellington.

(C) **VARIOUS:**

(i.) Most towns, boroughs, etc., have town plans on a large scale, showing streets, public services, etc.

(ii.) A few areas, of importance for either strategic or training purposes, have been mapped by the Defence Department; all topographical details are included. These are the only maps published with a military grid. Some of these have been placed on sale.

(iii.) In some districts, notably Hawke's Bay, 20-chain and 40-chain contoured topographical maps have been prepared, but not printed. These can be inspected (where they are available) at the Lands and Survey Department Office. They have been drawn from aerial surveys. Tracings from these are excellent training and operational maps.

(iv.) Automobile Association route maps are the best road maps for transport purposes. They give full information about road surfaces, gradients, etc. Every unit should make a point of having the local road maps available.

2—Reading and Use of Maps.

(A) Training in the use of maps has for its object the teaching of a man—

(i.) To visualize quickly and correctly the features represented on a map.

(ii.) To discover his position in any area for which he has a map.

(iii.) To use a map to determine road gradients, intervisibility of points, suitable routes, tactical positions, etc.

B) The first requirement is to be able to understand the conventional representation of objects.

(i.) The first thing to examine is the **scale.** This is expressed in two ways:—

(a) E.g., 4ins. equal 1 mile. This means that a line 4ins. long on the map represents a distance of one mile.

(b) By the **representative fraction** or **R.F.** This is the fraction that the distance between the points on the map is of the distance between the corresponding points on the ground, e.g., a scale of 1in. to 1 mile has an R.F. of 1/63,360, because 1 inch on the map represents a distance of 63,360ins. (i.e., 1 mile) on the ground. It follows that multiplying a distance measured on the map by the denominator of the R.F. will give the real distance. This is useful when the scale expressed as in (a) is in unfamiliar units, e.g., "1 centimetre to 1 kilometre."

A map drawn on a small scale is one which represents a big distance on the ground by a small length on the map (e.g., 1in. to 100 miles). A **large scale** is one which represents a distance on the ground by a relatively larger length on the map (e.g., 8ins. to 1 mile, a large scale for a topographical map).

(ii.) If the map is being used in the area it represents, especially in the field, the map should then be **set or orientated,** i.e., it should be placed so that directions on the map correspond with the directions they represent. This may be done in several ways:—

(a) By means of the compass (see Section B I, p. 98).

(b) By using easily recognisable points, etc., e.g., roads, a railway, towns, prominent hills.

(iii.) **Towns,** roads, railways, rivers, etc., are shown by unambiguous signs, which may vary from map to map.

(iv.) **Relief** is shown in various ways -

(a) In the absence of any direct representation the direction of the rivers will give a rough indication of the direction of intervening hills and spurs. On most maps the trig. stations have heights shown, and the heights of other points may also be given. These **"spot heights"** will give an indication of the steepness of the country.

(b) **Hachuring,** the drawing of short straight lines along the direction of the steepest slope, i.e., the direction in which water would run, is commonly used in manuscript maps; and some form of **shading** (shading in one side of a range or spur, and leaving the other light, for example) is used in printed maps.

(c) The only full and accurate way to show the details of relief is by **contour lines.** These are lines joining all points at the same height above sea-level. Depending on the scale of the map, the height between successive contour lines will vary from 50ft. to 1000ft. This height, known as the **"vertical interval"** or **"V.I.,"** should be shown on all contoured maps. Passing, on the map, from the 300ft. contour to the 400ft. one is obviously going uphill. The **gradient** of the slope is obtained by measuring the distance apart, as shown by the scale on the map, of the two contour lines, and dividing the V.I. by this, e.g., the distance apart of the 600ft. and 700ft. contours where they cross a road may be 40 chains. The gradient there will therefore be 100ft./40 chains = 100/2640

$$= \text{gradient of 1 in 26.4.}$$

It follows that contour lines close together represent a steep slope; far apart, a gentle slope.

When contour lines bend they represent either a valley or a spur. If the heights shown by the lines increase from the outside to the inside of the bend, it shows a spur; if they decrease, a valley. A **section,** or outline of the relief along a certain

92

line on the map, can be obtained by laying the edge of a sheet of paper along the line, and marking on the edge the points where the contour lines are cut by the edge of the paper, and against each the height represented. If from the points so marked lines are drawn at right angles to the edge to any suitable scale to represent the heights of the contour lines, and the tops of these lines joined by smooth curves, the joining line will give a representation of the surface. It must be remembered that unless the lines at right angles to the edge of the paper are drawn on the same scale as the map, the gradients will be exaggerated, but a section drawn on any scale will enable the intervisibility of two points to be decided. If a straight line joining two points on the section cuts the section, the points cannot be seen from each other; if it does not, they can.

(d) In sketch maps, if there is no time for the field work required for contouring, rough contours drawn by eye, called "form-lines," are sometimes used.

C) FINDING ONE'S POSITION ON, A MAP.

One's position on a map may be found in two ways:—

(i.) With a compass (see Sec. 3B ii., p. 99).

(ii.) Without a compass, by **resection.** First, three points on the map must be recognised on the ground. Place a piece of transparent paper on a level surface, and mark a point near the centre. This point represents your position. Without disturbing the paper draw from this point rays in the directions of the three recognised points on the ground. Place the transparent paper on the map and twist it about until you get the three rays to pass through the three points on the map that correspond to the points on the ground to which they were drawn. The rays may have to be extended to do this. When this is done, the original point on the paper will be over your position on the map.

(D) MAP REFERENCES.

Positions on the ground can be best described by **map references.** These can be:—

(a) Distance and bearing from some easily recognised reference point.

(b) Bearings from two easily recognised points. An inaccurate method if a prismatic compass is to be used to obtain the bearings.

(c) A **grid reference,** a method of describing a point on a map by means of a set of figures. As no two points on a map can have the same grid reference, this is a method of obviating mistakes. There are few areas in New Zealand of which there are maps gridded on the military grid system, but all civil maps of this country are, or can easily be gridded according to the civil grid system. Both systems are explained below only in so far as they will be required by Guardsmen for a working knowledge of the maps of the country.

(i.) **Military Grid System:** The present system is the Modified British System. On looking at a military map of, say, 1 inch = 1 mile, it will be seen to be overprinted with a series of horizontal and vertical lines thus forming a number of squares. In the margins will be found figures giving each line a value of so many kilometres north (horizontal) of a certain point of reference. Usually the last two figures only are given, but every 10 kilometres the full figure is given, e.g., 460. For the purpose of giving a grid reference, only the last two figures are used. When required to find a point on a map whose grid reference is, say, 6224, proceed as follows:—Divide the reference in half, 62 — 24. Now from the left-hand bottom corner of the map proceed horizontally to the right until reaching the vertical line with a value of 62. Again from the left-hand bottom corner move vertically until reaching the horizontal line of 24. The intersection of these two lines is the reference 6224. It will be seen that this point is the left-hand bottom corner of one of the small squares, and the whole square or any point in the square may be referred to by the reference 6224. When it is desired to refer to a point inside this small square, one divides this square into 100 still smaller squares, i.e., ten divisions east, and ten north. By regarding this as a demical place it will readily be seen that a reference 625245 will be in the exact centre of this square.

In orders, reports, etc., one specifies at the top left of the report the map used, and all places named in the body of the report are followed by their reference, e.g., RED HOUSE 857935.

On some military maps the lines are 1000 yards apart instead of 1 kilometre.

(ii.) **Civil Grid System:** As this system is likely to be more used by Guardsmen in this country it will be explained in slightly more detail.

New Zealand is divided into a number of Circuit Districts (e.g., Hawke's Bay and Wellington Circuit Districts), the geographical centre of that district being taken as the reference point "A" for that district.

Each of the Circuit Districts is divided into a number of Survey Districts each 1000 by 1000 chains. There are 44 Survey Districts in the Hawke's Bay Circuit District. Each of these Survey Districts is subdivided into sixteen squares 250 by 250 chains, called Blocks, which are numbered I. to XVI.

In the military system, where the reference point is bottom left, references are given as east and north only. In the civil system, where the reference point is in the centre of each district, a reference may be north and east, south and east, south and west, or north and west.

On looking at a map with the civil grid printed on it, one will note that the horizontal and vertical lines are marked giving the number of chains north or south, and east or west of the point "A" for that district. The lines are 100 chains apart. On the 20 chains to 1 inch maps (large scale maps of most use to Guardsmen) these large squares will be 5 inches by 5 inches.

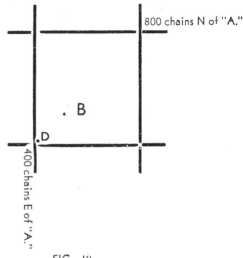

800 chains N of "A."

400 chains E of "A."

.D

. B

FIG. 19.

The reference to point D is 700 N

400 E

The reference to point B is 725 N

425 E

This system is at least as accurate as the military system, and is the system preferred by specialists. It will probably be the system used by the Home Guard.

3—Prismatic Compass.

(A) THE COMPASS.

(i.) The magnetic needle of the usual compass in the case of a service compass carries a card, divided into 360°. When the needle is at rest. 0° (or 360°, which is the same point) is pointing to the magnetic north. In

New Zealand this is, in 1941, approximately 17° 30′ east of true north. The degrees read from north through east to south, i.e., clockwise. East is then 90°, S.W. is 225°, and so on.

(ii.) The **"bearing"** of a distant point is found by turning up the prism and the hinged lid and holding the compass with the left thumb through the ring, so that the right eye looks into the prism. The slit above the prism and the hair line on the cover are aligned on the object, and its bearing is read through the prism on the card, when this has been brought to rest.

(iii.) To check the swing of the dial, the check-stud, protruding from the case to the left of the hinge lid, is pressed, as nearly as possible at the middle of the swing of the dial. It is released, and the dial again checked in mid-swing, until the dial finally comes to rest.

(iv.) It must be remembered that the compass gives magnetic bearings. To convert these to true bearings add 17° 30′, e.g., a compass bearing of 135° is a true bearing of 152° 30′; a compass bearing of 349° is a true bearing of 6° 30′.

(v.) Few prismatic compasses read correctly. Each compass varies by a certain amount from the true magnetic north, and this amount for any compass can only be found by taking a bearing with it along a north and south line set out by a surveyor or other competent man by means of a standard compass. This variation is called the **compass error.** In converting compass bearings to true bearings compass error, if appreciable, must be taken into account, e.g.—

(a) A compass bearing is 176°. It is known that the magnetic variation is 17° 30′ E., and that, if a bearing is taken along a true north line with this particular compass, the bearing read will be 344° 30′, i.e., the compass has an "error" of 2°, and the magnetic north as shown by this compass is 2° W. of its real position. The **true** bearing is easily found by a diagram.

97

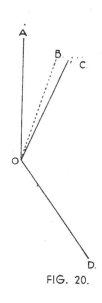

FIG. 20.

OA is the true north.

OD is the direction of the bearing 176°.

From OB, the direction in which the compass reads 0° to OD is 176°.

From OA to OC is 17° 30′, the magnetic variation.

From OB to OC is 2°, the compass error.

The true bearing of OD is then clearly 176° (compass bearing) +17° 30′ (magnetic variation) −2° (compass error) = 191° 30′.

(B) If the compass error were in the opposite direction it would be added as the following diagram shows:

The angle AOD, the true bearing, is the sum of the angles AOC (magnetic variation), COB (compass error) and BOD (compass bearing).

FIG. 21.

(B) **THE USE OF THE COMPASS.**

(i.) To set a map, open the compass lid right back and lay it on the map so that the hair line lies along the line of magnetic north on the map. Then turn map and

compass together till the arrow of the compass is pointing along the hair line. The map is then orientated.
On most New Zealand maps no line of magnetic north
is given, and often no north line, but there is a dotted
grid, the vertical lines of which are true north lines.
To set the map using a true north line, lay the compass
as above with the hair line along a true north line, and
turn map and compass until the arrow points to the
bearing of magnetic north (i.e., 17° 30′ in 1941).

(ii.) To take bearings for the purposes of—

    (a) **Field sketches** (see Sec. 5B, p. 102).

    (b) **Resection,** i.e., finding one's position on a map,
        bearings to three prominent points, roughly 60°
        apart, are taken, and from these points **back bear-
        ings** (i.e., the bearings plus 180°, remembering that
        a bearing over 360° is east of north again, so 360°
        is subtracted), converted to true bearings, are
        plotted on the map. Where the three lines so
        drawn intersect will be your position.

(iii.) To set the compass in order to march at night on a
given bearing, loosen the milled screw on the side of
the case and turn the glass cover until the luminous
patch is set at the required bearing, read on the scale
engraved on the outside of the case. Tighten up the
screw to prevent the cover moving. The bearing at
night is obtained by turning the compass until the
luminous arrow points to the patch on the cover. The
line of march is then obtained by sighting through the
slit on to the two luminous patches on the lid. To make
more certain of this direction a piece of string with a
peg at each end may be stretched alongside the
compass in the direction of the bearing.

(C) CAUTION.

The magnetic needle is very sensitive to iron, and to
other magnetised bodies. In taking bearings, make sure
no rifles, tanks, or artillery are within 50 yards; if possible, avoid wire fences, railway lines, water pipes, and
other men with compasses. Carry no iron tools, pocket
knives or enamelware.

4—Plane Table.

The plane table has several advantages over the compass for many purposes, but for active service it is not so useful, being bulky and not capable of being used effectively from cover. Plotting with a plane table is quicker, being done directly in the field.

(A) **EQUIPMENT:** The equipment consists of:—

(a) A **Drawing Board,** 18in. to 24in. square.

(b) A **Tripod** to which the board is fixed in such a way that it can be rotated after being levelled on the tripod by means of the spirit level.

(c) A **Sight Vane,** sometimes called a **Sight Rule** or **Alidade,** made of flat wood 12in. to 15in. long, 1½in. to 2in. wide. The sides should be true and parallel, and the edges bevelled, to allow straight lines to be ruled. At one end is a folding brass vane, with a vertical slit in the middle; at the other, the front, a similar vane with a vertical hair-line in the slit (horse-hair, waxed thread, or thin wire can be used).

(d) A **Spirit Level.**

This outfit can be improvised. The drawing board need not be surfaced if it is covered with heavy cardboard. The tripod can be a camera tripod, or can even be dispensed with by fixing the board to a box, although rotating and levelling in this case is made much more difficult. Ingenuity will devise ways of fixing the board to the stand so that rotation and then clamping is possible. The sight rule is easily made, using three-ply or 1/16in. sheet metal for the folding vanes.

(B) **USE OF PLANE TABLE.**

(i.) A sheet of paper is pinned to the board. A prominent landmark in the area to be mapped is chosen as one end of a base line (Station A) and the table is set up there, making sure with the spirit level that the surface of the board is horizontal.

(ii.) Make a dot on the paper to represent Station A, arranging it so that it will be related to the paper as the station is related to the area to be mapped.

(iii.) Hold a pencil, point downwards, on the dot, and bring one edge of the sight vane against it. Rotate the vane until the line of sight through the slit and the hair-line is on an object to be plotted, and draw a line along the edge of the vane that is against the pencil. It does not matter which edge is used, so long as the same edge is always used.

(iv.) Another prominent point, visible from A, and separated from A by ground over which distance can be paced or measured, is chosen as the other end of the base line, and its direction from A is plotted as in (iii.)

(v.) Before leaving A a number of rays to prominent objects is drawn, each being labelled with the object to which it points. All these rays will, of course, pass through the dot.

(vi.) The distance to Station B, the other end of the base line, is determined, and the corresponding length, according to the scale being used, is marked off on the ray drawn from A to B.

(vii.) The table is set up at B; the sight vane set along the line A B, and the board rotated until the line of sight through the slit and the hair-line is on Station A. Then the board is clamped.

(viii.) Rays are drawn from B with the sight vane to all the objects sighted from A, and the position of an object is given by the point of intersection of the rays to it from A and B.

(ix.) Further details will be found under Field Sketches, paragraph 5, below.

5—Field Sketches.

(A) Every Military Sketch should have on it:—

(i.) Descriptive heading or title, stating the general purpose of the sketch.

(ii.) True north and Magnetic north points, with the value of the magnetic variation shown. The top of the paper should as a rule be pointing towards true north; but this may be varied in a Road or River Traverse, in which the starting point would be shown at the bottom of the paper; or in the Sketch of a Position, in which the direction of the enemy would be shown at the top of the sketch.

(iii.) The Scale, between 4in. and 6in. long, and divided as detailed below in paragraph (C iv.).

(iv.) Statement of Scale (e.g., 1in.=8m.)

(v.) The R.F.

(vi.) The Vertical Interval (if the sketch is contoured).

(vii.) Signature, Rank and Unit.

(viii.) Date when sketch is made.

NOTES: (i.) The direction of rivers shown by an arrow.

(ii.) Roads labelled (to and from).

(iii.) Usual scales are:—

(a) For towns and villages, 12in. to 1m.

(b) For positions, 4in. to 1m.

(c) For route sketches, 1in. to 4in. to 1m.

(d) For tracts of country, 1in. to 4m.

(e) Sketches of fortifications should show a scale reading to 10 yards.

(f) A sketch for artillery should show 50 yards in secondary division of the scale.

(B) PACE AND COMPASS SKETCHING.

(i.) The sketcher should count the number of normal paces he takes to cover a measured 100 yards. Care must be taken in stepping this not to vary the normal pace.

(ii.) To sketch a tract of country:—

(a) Choose two points, visible from each other, separated by ground over which you can pace accurately, as far apart as conveniently possible, and preferably within the area to be mapped.

(b) From each point take bearings to a number of prominent and unmistakable objects. Plot the base line and the objects roughly in the field. The intersection of the bearings to an object from the two points will give its position when the sketch is drawn out to scale.

(c) Points between these prominent objects can be placed by a combination of pacing and bearings; and finer detail still sketched in by eye with respect to the points accurately fixed.

(iii.) Road (or river) traverse—

    (a) From the starting point choose a prominent object on or near the road, and take its bearing.

    (b) Pace towards it in a straight line, placing points to right or left of the line by pacing or estimating their distances at right angles from the line, at so many paces along it from the starting point. This is called **offsetting**.

    (c) On reaching the object chosen, repeat the proceedings as from the starting point.

    (d) Work round bends and curves by going from object to object in straight lines, offsetting the curves at intervals as frequent as may be required to plot the curve with some degree of accuracy.

(iv.) Only details of military importance should be included in the sketch.

(v.) The sketch should not be obscured by too much wording, and the wording should be printed, not written. Use conventional signs; but give a reference table with every sketch, of the signs used.

'C) DRAWING THE SKETCH FROM FIELD OBSERVATIONS.

(i.) Lay down the true north direction, usually parallel to the side of the paper, with a star at the north end, and across it draw a line at the correct angle showing the direction of magnetic north, putting an arrow at the northern end.

(ii.) Choose a point on the paper roughly corresponding to the position of one end of the base line in the area mapped.

(iii.) Through this point draw a line parallel to the true north, and lay off from the line the **true** bearing (i.e., magnetic bearing as read in the field + the magnetic variation) of the other end of the base line.

(iv.) In a part of the paper that will not be occupied by the sketch (the lower right corner is usually convenient) draw a line of length to be determined as follows:

    (a) Sketching to a scale of 4ins. to 1 mile (R.F.= 1/15,840), a line 4.54ins. long will represent 2000 yards. If this is divided into five equal pieces each piece will represent 400 yards. To divide it, draw from one end, at an angle to the line, another line; mark off on this second line with dividers five equal lengths. Join the last dividing mark to the other end of the 4.54in. line, and through the other dividing marks draw lines parallel to this joining line. These five divisions on the scale-line so obtained are called the primary divisions. Divide in a similar way the first primary division into four equal divisions (secondary divisions) each of which then represents 100 yards, or into eight secondary divisions, representing 50 yards.

(b) Sketching to any other scale, a similar method is employed, taking care that the primary divisions represent some unit (such as 100 yards, 500 yards, etc.) that can easily be subdivided.

(c) Convenient scales for a sketch of a small area, which can be quickly drawn, are:—(i.) 16 inches to 1 mile, when 1in. represents 5 chains (R.F. 1/3960); (ii.) 1 inch to 100 yards (R.F. 1/3600).

(v.) Set off along the ray drawn in (c) above the distance shown on the scale as representing the length of the base line. The point so obtained represents the other end of the base line.

(vi.) Through this point draw a true north line, and from it lay off the bearings taken from the corresponding point in the field.

(vii.) Lay off the bearings from the other end of the base, and so obtain the positions of the major objects in the area.

(viii.) Using these points, plot by scale and protractor the secondary points, and fill in the minor details recorded in the field.

(ix.) It is important that, in field sketches, the sketcher should give on his map a table of the signs he has used and the meaning that is to be attached to them. These may be devised as needed to meet special requirement, but must be used consistently in the same map.

Roads:

(i.) Draw with continuous lines if they are fenced or lined by a ditch or any obstruction which would prevent troops moving freely on or off the road.

(ii.) With dashes or dotted lines if they are unfenced.

(iii.) It should be shown whether the road is metalled, or tar-sealed, and the width of the metalled, etc., surface should be shown at intervals along its length, e.g., "14'm" signifies that the road is 14ft. wide and metalled.

(iv.) A metalled (or better) road 14ft. wide will allow two lines of wheeled traffic.

Rivers:

(i.) If over 15ft. wide, show by double lines; if under, by a single line.

(ii.) An arrow denotes the direction of the current.

Railways:

A single continuous line with cross-bars is usual. The words "single" and "double" written along it will denote single or double tracks.

Bridges:

Should be neatly labelled to show their construction, e.g., "Concrete, two spans," etc.

Cuttings and Embankments:

Are shown by lines at right angles to the road or railway. A line is drawn round this hachuring, representing the lip, in the case of a cutting, and not in the case of an embankment.

(x.) Leave ample room at the top for heading, notes, etc.

(D) **PLANE-TABLE SKETCHING.**

The method of procedure is much as for pace and compass. A base line is chosen, stepped out, but plotted to scale on the paper. Bearings are replaced by rays drawn directly on the paper in the field. Plotting by "offsets" and by eye is carried out exactly as with the compass.

(E) **The Topographical or Cadastral Maps,** or tracings from them, can well be used as the basis of field sketches. In the course of map training use can be made of exercises in field-sketching to fill in topographical detail in these maps for use as operational maps in tactical exercises. The superimposing of a grid (not necessarily the military grid for the whole country) will make such maps of great value at all stages of training.

6—Enlarging.

(i.) A rectangle is lightly drawn in pencil on the map surrounding the area to be enlarged; its sides are divided into equal segments. By joining these across, the whole area is divided into equal small rectangles, preferably squares.

(ii.) If the scale is to be doubled, a rectangle with sides double those of the big one drawn on the map is laid out on the paper, and this is divided exactly as the one on the map was.

(iii.) Diagonal lines are then drawn so that the small rectangles on the map and on the paper are divided into four triangles.

(iv.) Points on the map are transferred rectangle by rectangle to the enlargement by noting their position with reference to the sides and diagonals, and plotting them in the same relative positions on the paper.

(v.) This work may be speeded up by making two frames of light wood or heavy cardboard, one double the dimensions of the other, with black thread laced through holes in the frame in the same pattern as the lines drawn on the map. Their purpose is exactly that of the lines as explained in (iv.) above.

7—Reconnaissance Reports.

Two kinds of Reconnaissance:

(1) Reconnaissance of an enemy position, his strength and disposition.

(2) Reconnaissance for collecting information regarding country, and its resources, or regarding camps, bivouacs, billets, railways, etc.

(A) PRELIMINARY REQUIREMENTS:

(i.) The officer or N.C.O. making the reconnaissance must understand the object of his report. He must have all the information that is available, and know exactly what further information is required. His report should be a series of answers to definite questions.

(ii.) If a map is available, this should be carefully studied.

and it should be decided whether a plan or field sketch is desirable to supplement the report. All the gear necessary for the reconnaissance should be assembled and checked before moving out.

(iii.) During the reconnaissance the questions to be answered must be borne in mind, and information not required must not clutter up the report. Information given must be definite, not vague; e.g., "The river is 40 yards wide," not "fairly wide."

(iv.) The essentials are:—
        (a) Clearness.
        (b) Conciseness.
        (c) Accuracy.

These are best obtained by a tabulated arrangement of the report under numbered headings and sub-headings.

(B) THE REPORT CONSISTS OF THREE PARTS:

    (1) A plan or sketch.
    (2) The report proper.
    (3) Tabulated details.

The report should be properly addressed, its purpose stated in the heading, it should be dated, and signed with the name and rank of the officer or N.C.O. making the report.

(C) EXAMPLES OF HEADINGS for Typical Reconnaissance.

(i.) **Attack:**
    Extent of enemy position, location and strength of flanks; disposition, entrenchments, wire, obstacles; suitable lines of advance, forming up places, observation posts, suitability of ground for A.F.V.,

(ii.) **Defence:**
    Extent of position to be defended, reserve positions, observation posts, field of fire, facilities for surprise, covered ways within the position, nature of the soil for digging, wire available locally, outpost position, buildings suitable for defence, best lines for counter-attack, lines for withdrawal, routes for supplies and communications, forming-up points for reinforcements, lines of approach for A.F.V.'s, suitable positions for road-blocks, water supply, etc.

107

(iii.) **Camping Grounds:**

> Extent, nature, shape, road, rail and sea approaches, water supply, cover from air, fuel, storage, power supply, etc.

(iv.) **Bridges:**

> Nature, span, dimensions, height above water, rail, and/or road, load that can be carried, etc.

(v.) **Country:**

> . Flat or hilly, open or closed, water supply, roads, railways, telephone and power lines, towns and villages, etc.

(vi.) **Fords:**

> Depth, nature of bottom, distance across, approaches, banks, etc.

(vii.) **Rivers:**

> Width, depth, current, bridges, fords, ferries, watering places, approaches, liability to flooding, tidal rise, navigability, boats available.

(viii.) **Roads:**

> Nature, surface, condition, width, gradients, suitability for M.T., fences, nature of ground on either side, defiles, etc.

(ix.) **Water Supply:**

> Streams, ponds, wells, flowing or stagnant, number of animals that can be watered at a time, fitness for drinking, yield in gallons per hour.

(D) **NOTES.**

(i.) **Water Supply:**

> On active service allow I gal. per man, and 5 gals. per per horse per day. In standing camps the minimum will be 5 gals. per man and I0 gals. per horse per day.

(ii.) **Billeting** (to form basis for a report on Billeting) :

> (a) In the absence of information, an area can be assumed to give full subsistence for one week to a body of troops twice the number of the inhabitants: without subsistence, in a rich agricultural district, for ten men to one of the population; in towns and industrial areas, for six men to one of the population.

(b) Neither bedding nor furniture can be demanded, but billets include attendance and the use of cooking utensils.

(c) Alarm posts must be detailed, and routes to assembly places reconnoitred. Lines of approach to assembly points of different units must not cross. There should be distinctive alarms for the air attack, gas, artillery, and for other forms of attack from the ground. Civilians are entitled to protection, and arrangements for these emergencies must include them.

(d) Billeting parties usually consist of one officer, one N.C.O., and one other rank from each company. The party calls on the local mayor and explains what is proposed. They then allocate the areas and the names of the officer and the number of men to go to each billet are chalked on the door. These marks must be removed before the unit leaves. Officers must be near their men, and men near their M.T. and guns. Staff officers near their officers. Both sides of the road should be allotted to the same unit. No vehicles must be parked on the main road.

(e) Medical units and H.Q. have first claim on any building. Guns and vehicles may be parked outside the house area to avoid congestion.

(f) When troops enter a village no information must be allowed to leak out to the enemy through civilians. All telephones and pigeons must be taken over.

(g) Officers are to inspect the billets of their men at irregular intervals, once by day and once by night. Arms are to be kept inside the buildings, and under armed guard.

(iii.) **Camps and Bivouacs:**
(a) Platoons should have set areas allotted to them with room for their transport if possible. Sites should be on dry ground, grassed if possible, with good entrances and exits, and water supply at hand.

(b) Careful organization is necessary to have units close to the positions they will have to defend if attacked.

(c) Cookhouse, ablution points, drainage and latrines must be carefully planned and laid out.

(E) PANORAMA AND DRAWINGS.

A conventional reproduction on paper of the view obtained by an observer from a given point will often be a valuable addition to a reconnaissance report.

(i.) The principles to be observed in making a panorama are:—

(a) The ground must be studied carefully with the naked eye and with binoculars.

(b) The principles of perspective must be followed as far as possible.

(c) The drawing must be simple. No line should be drawn without a definite idea of what that line is to represent, and of the necessity for it.

(d) All natural objects such as buildings, trees, hedges, etc., should be shown by conventional outline only.

(e) Firm continuous lines are to be used. Feathered and undecided lines must be avoided.

(ii.) The equipment required is:—A service protractor or a ruler, a length of string, a pencil capable of producing both a fine and a firm black line (an "H," say), a rubber, and suitable paper, preferably squared.

(iii.) Thirty degrees of arc is the maximum suitable area to draw on a single sheet. This can be gauged in the field by holding a ruler six inches long at about a foot from the eyes, and closing one eye.

(iv.) When the area to be sketched has been chosen, the outstanding points are plotted in their correct relative positions. This is done by holding the ruler at a constant distance from the eye and reading off on it the horizontal and vertical distances from a point of reference of the various points to be plotted (but see Sec. vii. below). The ruler is held at a constant distance by threading the string through a hole in it and tying knots at each end. One knot is held in the teeth, the other is kept tight against the ruler.

(v.) A simple device which will increase the speed of drawing can be made by taking a piece of heavy card, cutting out of the centre a rectangle 6ins. by 2ins.; a piece of photographic film, previously cleaned in warm water and quite clear, is then pasted over the hole, and a grid of half-inch squares is drawn on the celluloid. The effect thus obtained is that of a ruled celluloid window through which the landscape may be viewed. The paper is ruled in a similar way to the window. The frame is kept at a fixed distance by a string held in the teeth, and the detail seen can then be transferred square by square to the paper.

(vi.) Intermediate points are then plotted by further measurements, or by eye. Fuller detail is then drawn in lightly and the whole sketch compared with the landscape. The work is then drawn in more firmly, bearing in mind that the pencil lines should become darker and firmer as they approach the foreground..

(vii.) It will usually be found that a vertical scale twice the horizontal scale will make possible the showing of small folds, etc. This relation of scales should be noted on the sketch.

(viii.) The panorama is completed by writing vertically, above the points, names of hills, roads, rivers, etc., and connecting the names with their representations in the sketch by vertical arrows. Ranges and map references should be given where possible.

(F) THUMBNAIL SKETCHES.

Small sketches of road intersections, as they will be seen by troops approaching from a certain direction, of fords, buildings for defence or demolition, detours in the road, etc., are valuable additions to a report. These are made on the same principles as the panorama sketches. In neither of these forms of sketching is artistic sense required, but practice is essential.

8—Intelligence.

(A) GENERAL.

(i.) **Time Factor:** The speed of modern warfare makes the time factor of the greatest importance in intelligence work. Unit reconnaissance must be rapid, and the information reported to the unit commander in sufficient time to be made use of. The commander in turn must send back all information, as it comes in, for collation by the Intelligence Officer at battalion H.Q.

(ii.) The rule must be: "As soon as you receive information, pass it on." This applies in both directions, up and down.

(iii.) To attain these ends, it will always be necessary to ensure that adequate means of rapid transmission are available.

(B) DUTIES IN UNITS.

The duties intelligence personnel are called upon to perform include:—

(i.) To organize the system of intelligence within the unit.

(ii.) To observe and report enemy movements and dispositions.

(iii.) To study the progress of the battle on the front and flanks of the unit, and to be prepared to give information on the disposition of his own unit and of neighbouring troops.

(iv.) To study the topography of the unit area, including lines of approach to and from the enemy position.

(v.) To collect, sift and collate intelligence reports emanating from within the unit, and to distribute the information so obtained.

(vi.) To study the information received from higher authority or neighbouring units, and to draw the attention of the unit commander to any items calling for attention.

(vii.) To ensure that the unit is kept supplied with up-to-date maps.

(viii.) To see that orders are carried out with regard to prisoners of war, captured documents and material.

(ix.) To supervise military security within the unit.

(x.) To keep intelligence records up to date.

(C) **THE BATTALION INTELLIGENCE OFFICER** is responsible—

   (i.) That no sub-unit commander lacks any available information.

   (ii.) That concise summaries and sketch maps are available as quickly as possible following a change in the situation.

   (iii.) That the situation map, from which sketch maps can be produced, is kept posted.

   (iv.) That a simple diary or log-book is kept, from which a summary, if required, can be produced later.

CHAPTER VIII.

Field Engineering.

1—General Considerations. 2—A Defensive System. 3—Protective
Works. 4—Obstacles. 5—Explosives.

1—General Considerations.

(A) (i.) **Speed** in construction of field works in close proximity
to the enemy is always essential. Time, labour, tools
and materials available will invariably be insufficient to
meet all demands. Work will often have to be carried
out in darkness.

It is therefore essential that all ranks should be
conversant with the general principles, and thoroughly
drilled in the methods, and that all work should be done
to a prearranged and organized plan.

(ii.) A system of organization of work should ensure:—
  (a) Control.
  (b) Speed.
  (c) Efficiency.

(a) Control is best obtained by using normal units, i.e.,
complete sections or platoons, with definite tasks
allotted to them.

(b) Speed depends on training and on keeping to a
well-rehearsed system in the execution of the work.

(c) Efficiency, i.e., the economical use of the resources
available, depends on good organization ensuring
that labour, tools and materials are in the right place
in the right quantities at the right time.

(B) **Duties** of officers concerned in the initiation and execution of
field works:—

(i.) Unit commander ordering the work to be done:
  (a) Reconnaissance.
  (b) Priority of work.
  (c) Instructions to officer in charge of work.
  (d) Arrangements for provision of men, tools, materials
  and transport.

(e) Arrangements for control and continuity of work.

(f) Provision of a covering party if necessary.

(ii.) Officer in charge of work:
  (a) Detailed reconnaissance.
  (b) Design.
  (c) Estimates.
  (d) Marking out of work.
  (e) Guides for working parties.
  (f) Explanation of work to officers in charge of working parties.
  (g) Correct execution of work.

(iii.) Officer (or N.C.O.) in command of working party:
  (a) Explanation of the work to his subordinates.
  (b) Allotment of tasks to, and disposal of, men on the work.
  (c) Ensuring that men have the necessary tools and materials.
  (d) The diligence of his men.
  (e) The discipline of the party.
  (f) The execution of the work in accordance with instructions.
  (g) Handing over of work, tools, and materials to the next party, or as instructed.
  (h) Withdrawal of the party on the completion of the work.
  (i) Action in the event of casualties.

(C) Reconnaissance:
  (i.) The officer ordering the work to be done will carry out the preliminary reconnaissance, accompanied if possible by the officer in charge of the work.
  (ii.) The officer in charge of the work will then make a detailed reconnaissance of the task, covering the following considerations:—
    (a) The work to be done, its nature and quantity, and the locality.
    (b) The design best suited to the requirements.
    (c) The labour required.
    (d) The time available, when the work can be begun, how long it will take.
    (e) Rendezvous, routes and guides.
    (f) Transport.

115

(D) **Preliminary Arrangements:**
　　(i.) If time is short, responsibility must be decentralized and more left to the initiative of subordinates.
　　(ii.) All work should be marked out before the arrival of the working party by pegs, tapes, etc., under the supervision of the officer in charge of the work.
　　(iii.) Estimates based on the detailed reconnaissance must be made. No more men should be asked for than are absolutely necessary.

(E) **Organization of Working Parties:**
　　(i.) The efficiency of the party will depend on discipline and the allotment of suitable tasks.
　　(ii.) The advantage of task work over time work lies in the moral effect due to—
　　　　(a) Knowing what is to be done.
　　　　(b) Knowing that there is no chance of going until it is done.
　　(iii.) It is essential that tasks should be set fairly. They should be set for small parties rather than for individuals. They should take just less than the period of work (generally four hours) to complete. The nature of the soil must be considered in this connection.
　　(iv.) The whole task must be covered by the separate tasks set. This implies very full and careful planning.
　　(v.) A relief, if possible, should arrive complete with tools. It is impossible to hand over tools on the task in darkness. Failing this, one party should dump their tools in a convenient place for the relief to pick them up.
　　(vi.) Care must be taken that tracing marks of work to be done are concealed from enemy observation. A tracing party should rehearse its work beforehand if possible, to add to the speed with which it will be carried out.
　　(vii.) It is important that on arrival at the site of work the party should be distributed along the line of the work without noise or confusion. Practice is essential. The nature of the work and task must be explained to the party beforehand.
　　(viii.) Carrying parties must be organized as for working parties. The tools, etc., should be arranged in loads before the arrival of the party. The men must be told

the composition of the load before they start collecting them.

(ix.) If casualties are probable and various kinds of stores are being carried, the stores of any one kind should be distributed among different individuals.

(x.) Arms and equipment will usually be laid out behind the work, readily available in case of emergency. If there is no danger of attack, i.e., in a rear position, they will be left in a convenient spot under guard.

(x.) The procedure must be modified to meet all conditions.

2—A Defensive System.

(A) (i.) The object of the defence is to wear out the enemy and to gain time. The defence is assisted by making the best use of the ground, reinforced by the artificial aid of field works.

(ii.) The principles of defensive action are set out in Chapter X.

(iii.) The defensive action should be fought in advance of localities the retention of which is vital to the defender.

(iv.) Infantry positions will be sited wherever possible in localities protected from tank action.

(v.) The flanks should be naturally strong.

(vi.) Surprise is as important in defence as in attack. The position should therefore afford facilities for concealment.

(vii.) There should be ample room and good communications within and in rear of the position for manoeuvring reserves. and the ground should afford facilities for counter-attacks.

(B) Reconnaissance:

(i.) The reconnaissance and siting of the coastal defensive systems to be held by the Home Guard will be carried out by area commanders in conjunction with the Army. Battalion commanders will then make their dispositions in accordance with the general plan. If this work is put in hand early there will be ample time for units to know their defensive positions thoroughly and to rehearse their parts in the defensive scheme.

(ii.) A plan or several alternative proposals should be prepared for each locality after consideration of the tactical features, observation, lines of approach, and ground which must be denied to the enemy in a withdrawal. The approximate line for each stage at which it is proposed to hold the enemy will be marked on the map.

(iii.) For detailed reconnaissance for field works see Section IC above.

(C) Organization of a Defensive System:

(i.) All defensive systems should be planned from the outset so that they can easily be adapted to the requirements of a long defence.

(ii.) The first essential is to decide on the general line in front of which it is intended to stop the enemy. All defensive preparations will be based on the defence of this line. The troops will be distributed so that they can most effectively develop the fire power of their weapons. This will result in the holding of a chain of localities mutually supporting each other.

(iii.) Infantry defence localities will be sited in depth, and will consist of a series of defended posts manned by sections. The posts will consist of short lengths of fire trench, allowing five to six feet for each man, from which all-round fire is possible (see Fig. 22). They in turn will mutually support each other, and be connected up as time permits laterally and from front to rear.

(iv.) Units in reserve will also occupy a series of defended posts, but probably more concentrated than in the case of forward units, and sited to allow movement from one to another under cover.

(v.) Posts which adequately protect the intervening ground with fire when observation is good may not be able to do so in fog or darkness, and it may be necessary to establish connecting posts to prevent the enemy penetrating the position.

(vi.) Dummy trenches, unexpected obstacles, well-concealed fire positions tend to mislead the enemy as to the real nature of the defence, and may cause him to deploy prematurely or in a false direction.

(vii.) The defence at the junction of units requires very careful siting and co-ordination.

(viii.) To cover areas of great importance or where heavy attacks are expected it is necessary to construct defences in greater depth. In such cases one or more rear systems will be constructed at such distances behind the system in front that the enemy will be forced to move his artillery and organize a fresh offensive. Such rear systems will be organized as described above with a forward and a main zone.

(D) Defended Posts and Localities:

(i.) These are self-contained defence works, whether they are detached defences protecting some isolated point, or whether they are the groups of trenches or defended localities forming the framework of a complete defensive system.

(ii.) Defended posts are held by a section. They must be designed and sited to bring fire to bear in any required direction, especially over the ground in front of neighbouring posts. They must be wired and provided with observation posts. and be capable of all-round defence. Storage must be provided for water, rations, tools and ammunition. (See diagram, and also Section 3E, Weapon Pits, below.)

(iii.) Defended localities are areas organized for defence by definite units such as a platoon or a company.

Accommodation for the reserve must be provided in rear or on the flanks, and for ammunition, water, etc., in addition to any storage within the posts.

(iv.) Obstacles must be provided in the front and flanks, and where necessary in the rear, with gaps left for counterattacks. These gaps must be concealed from observation, and must be adequately covered by fire.

DEFENDED LOCALITY IN ISOLATED POSITION FOR 4 PLATOONS.

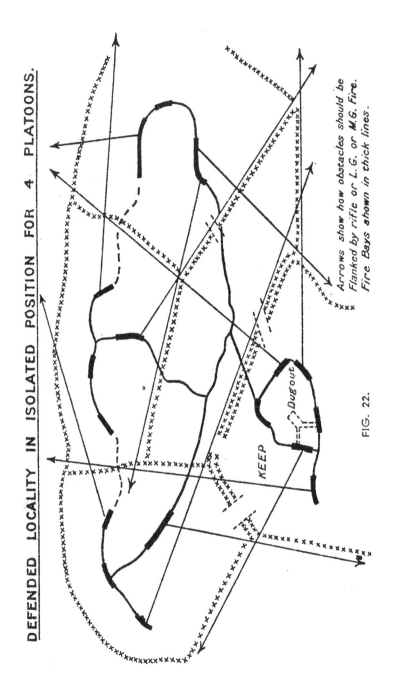

Arrows show how obstacles should be
Flanked by rifle or L.G. or M.G. Fire.
xxx Fire Bays shown in thick lines.

KEEP

Dugout

FIG. 22.

(E) Defence of Woods:

(i.) The inclusion of wooded areas in a defended locality depends on their situation and extent. Woods of small extent may be converted into obstacles to break up the attack by entangling their outer edges with wire, and siting trenches to flank them.

(ii.) If they are of large extent it will be advisable to include them if possible because—

(a) They afford cover for reserves, stores, etc.

(b) They give cover from tank attacks.

(c) If the enemy is allowed to occupy them they will cover concentrations of troops.

(iii.) The position of trenches in a wood should be far enough from the edge to prevent artillery ranging on the front and affecting the garrison. Wide clearings will have to be made in order to obtain a field of fire, and these clearings must be flanked by fire trenches. In extensive woods wide rides through them should be cut, and trenches sited to enfilade them.

(iv.) Passages within the wood must be cut to assist communications and plenty of direction boards provided so that any part of the defences can be reinforced without losing direction.

(F) Field Defences of Coast Lines:

(a) (i.) Works intended to resist the attack of a landing force will be sited with a view to obtaining the best fire effect while the enemy is approaching in boats or in the act of landing.

(ii.) Generally speaking, the system of defence should be one of mutually defended posts by which troops may be economized. Any advanced trenches which may be found necessary must be definitely affiliated to defended locality.

(iii.) Special attention should be paid to establishing road-blocking posts to command the junctions of roads leading from the coast, to ensure that fast-moving troops, cyclists, etc., may be prevented from penetrating.

(iv.) The development of a defensive system behind the defences on the coast will follow the principles set out above.

(b) The coast line may be classed under the following heads:

    (i.) Shingle beaches.

    (ii.) Sand hills.

    (iii.) Marshy shores with sea walls.

    (iv.) Clay cliffs.

    (v.) Rocky cliffs.

    (vi.) Town fronts.

(i.) **Shingle Beaches:** The chief difficulties these present are:

    (a) The ever-varying nature of the beach.

    (b) The risk of casualties caused by the shingle under artillery or machine-gun fire.

A shifting beach makes impossible the fixing of wire obstacles below the tide mark, and may obliterate defensive works. A position on this type of coast therefore calls for the highest order of vigilance on the part of its garrison.

The defences should be of the simplest nature: trenches should be sited on the crest of the shingle bank; obstacles of a portable nature should be made and held in reserve to supplement permanent obstacles. Sandbags filled with sand or earth should be stored at definite places to rectify small changes in the height of parapets and to give protection against flying shingle.

(ii.) **Sandhills:** Positions among sandhills have disadvantages similar to those on a shingle beach, with the additional difficulties caused by wind-blown sand. They have obvious advantages in their facilities for cover, and concealment of troops moving.

The defences are sited to bring the greatest fire to bear on the foreshore to prevent the enemy establishing a bridgehead. For if he can do so, he has the same advantages as the defence.

(iii.) **Marshy Shores with sea walls** are seldom met in New Zealand. They will have poor road communication and are unlikely points for a landing. They will require a less dense defence than other types.

(iv.) **Clay Cliffs:** The constant slipping will render occupation of the face dangerous and even impossible. The main system of defence should consist of a continuous entanglement on the top of the cliff with defended posts close to it. Material for obstacles should be stored in the vicinity for establishing trenches on the lower slopes if the necessity arises, but permanent positions cannot be established. Access to these lower positions should be arranged for. Every opportunity to develop cross fire from the top of the cliffs on the water and beach below must be seized.

(v.) **Rocky Cliffs:** However inaccessible a cliff may appear it should never be assumed to be so. Where it is impossible to obtain effective fire over the foreshore, defended posts must be established at the heads of all ravines debouching on to the shore, and arrangements made to ensure that the line of cliffs is watched. Fire positions on a cliff line are deceiving, for the area rendered dangerous to the enemy is comparatively small as a result of the plunging nature of the fire.

(vi.) **Town fronts** are usually strong against frontal attack because of the cover afforded to the defenders by the buildings from which the esplanade can be swept. A sea wall will afford an obstacle to an advance from the beach, especially if its top is wired. The flanks should be protected in the usual way. Portable obstacles should be ready to hand to block ramps leading to the beach and roads leading inland if necessity arises.

3—Protective Works.

(A) PRIORITY OF WORK.

(i.) There will never be time, labour or material enough to carry out all the useful work demanded. Careful selection will always be necessary.

(ii.) A comprehensive scheme of development must be planned from which a sequence of the work to be done will be drawn up, concentrating first on the essential minimum of each type of work.

(iii.) The following order of priority may be taken as a

general guide, but no hard-and-fast rule can be laid down:—

(a) Siting of weapons and observation posts.
(b) Improving communications.
(c) Improving field of fire.
(d) Digging fire positions and O.P.'s.
(e) Creating obstacles.
(f) Constructing shelters.
(g) Completing and connecting up fire positions.
(h) Completing the communication or connecting trenches.

(B) **CONCEALMENT.** (See also Chapter VI., Section 4.)

(i.) Concealment is always directed against two dangers:—
(a) Air observation.
(b) Ground observation.

It must be remembered that what is concealed from the air may be visible from the ground and vice versa.

(ii.) The chief ways of obtaining concealment are:—
(a) Screening.
(b) Blending.
(c) Deceiving.

(a) **Screening** involves making use of natural features, as well as artificial screens. These need not be solid to be effective. They are made of scrim, sacking, or wire-netting threaded with strips of canvas or branches. Their outlines should be irregular. Their colours should blend with the background. They must not restrict the view of the defenders.

(b) **Blending** is true concealment: it implies the avoidance of straight lines, unnatural colours, tone, shadows, etc., or the repetition of stereotyped works. A dark background broken by small patches of light affords the best concealment.

(c) **Deceiving** implies the construction of dummy works, erecting of dummy screens, laying down of dummy tracks. Dummy trenches need be only 1ft. to 18ins. deep, but the spoil must be thinly spread.

SNIPER'S POST.

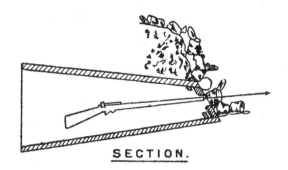

SECTION.

VIEW FROM FRONT.

When front parapet is covered with tins of all kinds, the tin used to disguise the loophole is very difficult to identify even at 10 yds. range

OBLIQUE LOOPHOLE.

Fire lying or standing.

FIRE STEP

Sniper's Post

FIRE STEP

TRAVERSE

Plenty of Dummy Loopholes should be provided.

FIG. 23—AN EXAMPLE OF CONCEALMENT.

(C) OBSERVATION.

(i.) Just as it is necessary for the defence to conceal themselves, so it is necessary to make it difficult for the
attacking troops to conceal themselves. A careful choice
of position will be the first consideration.

(ii.) Clearance of fields of view and fire will help, but
unintelligent clearance will give away a defended position, so clearance must be kept to a minimum.

(iii.) The valuable element of surprise in fire must not be
lost. Concealed positions with a restricted field of fire
are as a rule more effective than unconcealed positions
with a perfect field of fire.

(iv.) Any clearance should be done in the early stages of
the work. Where possible, results should be studied from
the enemy's point of view.

(v.) There are two objects for clearance:—
        (a) For observers.
        (b) For weapons.

For (a) more clearance will be necessary, but O.P.'s
should be so sited as to require as little as possible.

For (b) it will not be necessary to clear away everything. Hedges, lines of trees, bushes, if left standing,
help to screen our fire positions from enemy observers.
They can often be made into useful obstacles by wiring.
Clearing the lower part of a hedge will give an adequate
field of fire without sacrificing concealment.

(vi.) (a) **Trees** give more cover to the enemy when cut down
than when standing. Cut away the lower branches
if they are causing obstruction.

(b) **Bush:** Areas covered with thick bush cannot be
cleared. Clearings or lanes should be made, these
enfiladed, and the edges of the bush left should be
filled with obstacles.

(c) **Buildings:** If they are wooden they can be burnt; if
of concrete or brick, they should be gutted if necessary to prevent the enemy using the upper floors.

(d) **Crops:** High crops like wheat or maize cannot be
completely cleared. They should be treated like
bush, except that the lanes can be made either by
cutting or by marching a body of men through them.

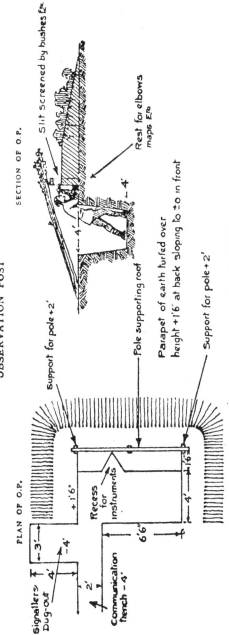

OBSERVATION POST

SECTION OF O.P.

Slit Screened by bushes &c

Rest for elbows
maps &c

Pole supporting roof

Parapet of earth turfed over
height +1'6" at back sloping to ±o in front

Support for pole +2'

Support for pole +2'

PLAN OF O.P.

+1'6"

Recess
for
instruments

Signallers
Dug-out
-3'
-4'
4'
2'

Communication
trench -4'

6'6"

4'

1'6"

4'

4'

NOTE.—A splinterproof roof should be added if time permits.

FIG. 24.

(D) COMMUNICATIONS.

    (i.) Improvement of communications within a position can be of great assistance, in saving time and fatigue.

    (ii.) Work may be necessary for:—

        (a) Tasks of reserves.

        (b) Passage of. runners.

        (c) Routine movements of men, carrying rations, etc.

        (d) Evacuation of casualties.

    (iii.) Single tracks, with gaps through hedges and means of crossing ditches will meet most of the above, but all obstacles to the movement of reserve troops along pre-arranged routes must be removed.

    (iv.) Tracks should be kept to a minimum. If there is danger of observation from the air, dummy tracks should be made.

    (v) Tracks should be signposted, and should be easily recognizable by night.

    (vi.) Routes for night patrols forward of the defended area should be given recognizable marks, but these must not be visible to the enemy.

(E) WEAPON PITS AND SECTION POSTS.

    (i.) **Parapet:**

        (a) At least 5ft. thick at the top to give protection from S.A. fire.

        (b) The closer the top of the parapet is to ground level the easier it is to conceal, but a minimum of 18ins. is usually necessary. If the parapet is lower than this it may be difficult to dispose of the spoil.

        (c) The top should not be flat and even, but as irregular as possible. It should slope gently towards the front.

    (ii.) **Parados:**

        (a) This serves two purposes, to protect the firer from shell-bursts in the rear, and to form a background for the heads of men firing.

        (b) It should be bullet-proof if possible, but it must be higher than the parapet, and should have approximately the same slope.

(iii.) **Elbow Rest:** The space between the foot of the parapet or parados and the edge of the trench.

    (a) It should never be less than 12ins. wide.

    (b) It is essential to prevent excavated earth falling into the trench.

NORMAL SECTION OF FIRE TRENCH

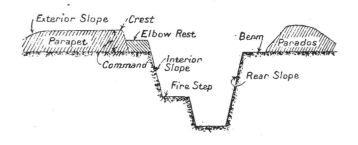

ORDER OF WORK.

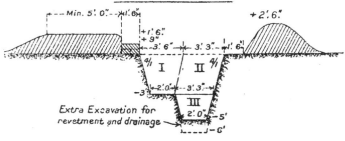

FINAL SECTION OF TRENCH.

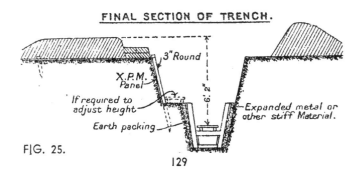

FIG. 25.

(iv.) **Firestep:**

    (a) It should be at least 2ft. wide, firm, and if possible revetted.

    (b) It should be normally 4ft. 6ins. below the top of the parapet.

    (c) On occupying a trench a man should at once test the parapet to make sure he can fire over it.

(v.) **Cross-Section:**

    (a) The sides are dug as steep as possible, but not steeper than 4/1, so that they will stand at any rate temporarily without being revetted.

    (b) The fire-trench must be wide enough to fire from comfortably, and will be widened later to allow walking behind the firers.

    (c) If time permits there should be a passage 2ft. wide behind the firestep.

(vi.) **Sequence of Digging Tasks** (see diagram).

    (a) A trench 3ft. 6ins. wide at the top, 2ft. at the bottom, and 3ft. deep is opened (I in the diagram). All the spoil is thrown forward to make the parapet, which even so will not be 5ft. thick.

    (b) The second stage (II in the diagram) is widened to 6ft. 6ins. at the top and 5ft. at the bottom, and the parapet completed before any earth is used for the parados. **It should never be deepened until it has been widened.**

    (c) Finally the passage-way shown as III in the diagram is dug, the earth going to the parados.

    (d) As soon as possible the firestep, and then the rest of the trench should be revetted, and a drainage channel dug.

(vii.) **Weapon Pits** are fire-trenches 6ft. long, to hold two or three men. They can be dug to the first stage in four hours by two men.

(viii.) **Section Posts:**

    (a) A series of weapon pits, three or four, arranged in such a way that all-round defence is possible. Four typical arrangements are shown, but the arrangements must be adapted to the site.

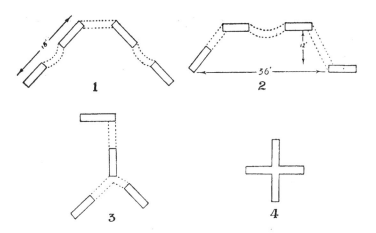

FIG. 26—TYPES OF SECTION POSTS.

The continuous lines are the weapon pits, the dotted lines crawl trenches.

Note.—No. 4 has obvious advantages for all-round defence in flat, open country.

(b) The weapon pits making up a post will, after being dug to stage I, be joined up by a **crawl trench** 3ft. 6ins. wide and 1ft. 6ins. deep. The spoil is thrown up as a parapet, but will afford cover from view only at this stage.

(c) After the weapon pit has reached stage III the crawl trenches will be widened and deepened. They should therefore make angles not less than 90 degrees nor more than 135 degrees with the weapon pits. This will give protection against enfilade fire, and will localize shell and bomb bursts.

(d) **Drainage** is of the greatest importance. If neglected, trenches will collapse in bad weather. Excavations of drains should be done uphill, and the bottom of the trench graded. If natural drainage cannot be effected sump-pits must be dug.

(e) **Latrines** should be constructed as early as possible. They are arranged for in small trenches off the weapon pits.

(ix.) **Breastworks** are made when it is impossible to obtain cover by digging trenches: for instance, in rocky country where there is no earth or in marshy country where the water lies on the surface. The trace and profile will follow the principles for trenches. They can be made of revetments or sandbag walls 10ft. apart at ground level, the space between being filled with earth.

(x.) **Revetting** can be carried out by—
(a) Sandbags.
(b) Hurdles of brushwood.
(c) Wire netting backed by sacking.
(d) Corrugated iron.

(xi.) **Slit Trenches:** A narrow trench, 18ins. wide and 2ft. deep, to hold one man, has several uses:—
(a) It gives quick protection from all types of fire.
(b) It will allow a tank to cross it without damage to its occupant.
(c) It gives sufficient protection for tank-hunters to throw Molotov Cocktails, etc.

F) SANDBAGS.

(i.) The service sandbag measures 33ins. by 14ins. when empty. These should be three-quarters filled and the neck tied round with string. The mouth should be tucked under when the bag is laid, and the corners tucked in. When laid it should measure 20ins. by 10ins. by 5ins.

(iii.) Grain bags or sacks can be used as substitutes for sandbags. They should not be more than half-filled or they are too heavy to handle. It is not necessary then to tie up the mouth if it is carefully folded under. The weight of the sack will prevent the loss of earth.

(iii.) Three men (two holding and tying, and one filling) can fill 60 bags an hour. Two men can lay 60 bags an hour.

SANDBAG REVETMENT.

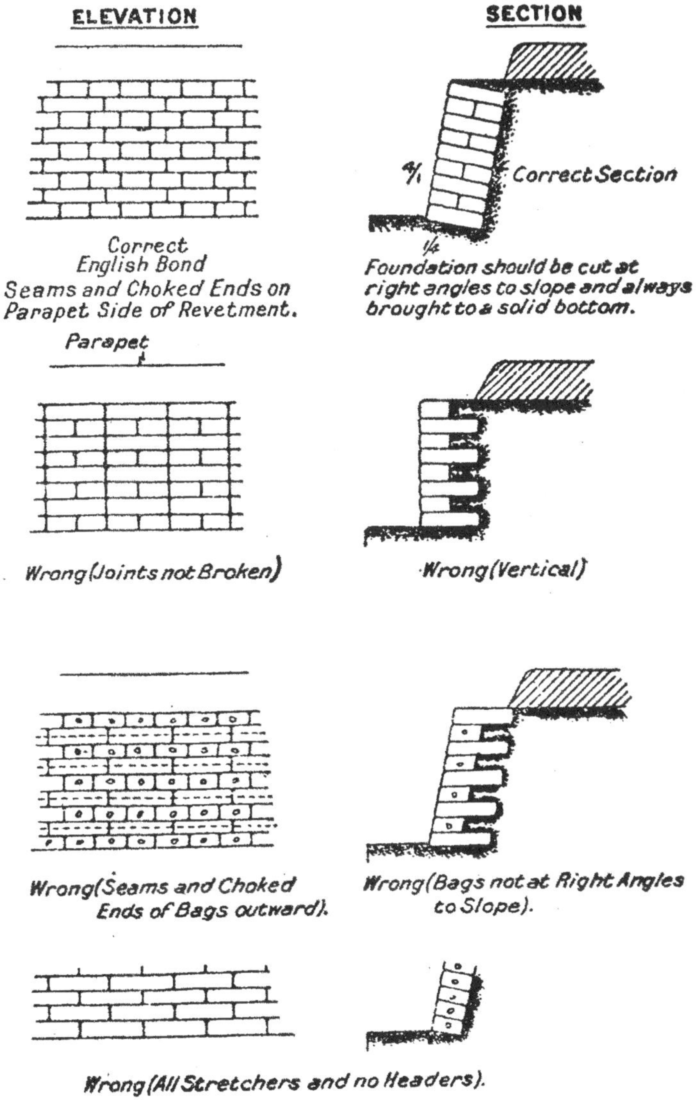

ELEVATION

SECTION

Correct Section

Correct
English Bond
Seams and Choked Ends on
Parapet Side of Revetment.

Foundation should be cut at
right angles to slope and always
brought to a solid bottom.

Parapet

Wrong (Joints not Broken)

Wrong (Vertical)

Wrong (Seams and Choked
Ends of Bags outward).

Wrong (Bags not at Right Angles
to Slope).

Wrong (All Stretchers and no Headers).

FIG. 27.

133

(iv.) To build a revetment to a trench wall, i.e., to line it to prevent loose earth or sand falling, a foundation is cut perpendicular to the slope and a wall of sandbags is built.

(v.) These are treated as bricks and built on the "English bond" system (see diagram). A bag is a "stretcher" when it is laid with its longest side parallel to the wall, and a "header" when it is at right angles to the wall.

(vi.) The chokes (tied ends) should be inwards in a header course, and if the stretcher has only one seam, this should also be inwards.

(vi.) The first course should be headers, followed by stretchers and headers alternately.

(viii.) A breastwork can be built with two sandbag walls 10ft. apart, the space between being filled with earth.

4—Obstacles.

(A) (i.) **General:** Obstacles may be either natural or artificial. The existence of natural obstacles will often be an important consideration in siting defences, which, in such cases, will be placed so as to cover the obstacles by fire. Natural obstacles are usually more effective against A.F.V. than artificial ones; although artificial obstacles sunk in ditches cannot easily be destroyed by tanks.

(ii.) **Characteristics of a Good Obstacle:**
    (a) Covered by fire.
    (b) Concealed.
    (c) Not giving away fire positions.
    (d) Irregular.
    (e) Strong.
    (f) Transparent.
    (g) Not obstructing the defence.

(B) **Wire Obstacles:** The best means of stopping infantry. Even a single strand will be a valuable aid in defence. Various types of entanglement are used:—

(i.) **Double Apron Fence:** Three horizontal wires fixed to the pickets, sloping wires (diagonals) from the tops of the

DOUBLE APRON ENTANGLEMENT.

AS FRAMEWORK FOR WIDE OBSTACLES.

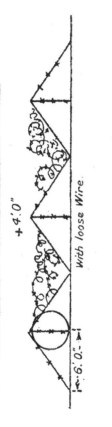

+ 4'.0"

With loose Wire.

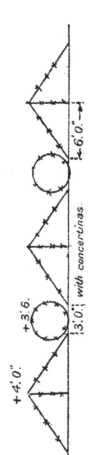

+ 3'.6.

:3'.0.: with concertinas.

+ 4'.0".

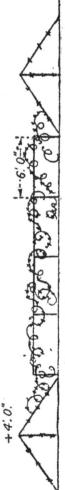

with knee high wire entanglements.

+ 4'.0".

FIG. 28.

pickets to the short pickets, and three horizontal wires fixed on each side to the diagonals.

(ii.) **Single Apron Fence:** Used if there is not time enough to complete a double apron. The front apron should be complete if possible.

(iii.) **Spider Wire:** Fences running in various directions with horizontal wires, without diagonals or aprons. Difficult to destroy with artillery. Not more than two or three fences should meet in a point. Can be used to fill in spaces between other wiring.

(iv.) **Concertinas:** Prepared beforehand (see Wiring Drill below). Quickly erected, but large carrying parties required, and the wire easily gets tangled in the dark.

(v.) **Knife Rests:** Two X's made of wood or iron, joined with spikes, or lashed with wire, fixed at the ends of a 10ft. to 15ft. pole, and strands of wire attached. The central pole should project at the ends, for carrying.

LARGE KNIFE REST MADE OF WOOD

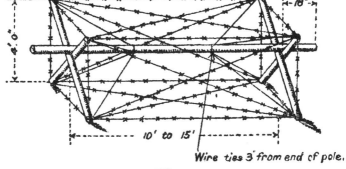

Wire ties 3' from end of pole.

FIG. 29.

(vi.) **Dannert Wire:** A new barbed wire made of a special spring steel, very difficult to destroy with artillery. Supplies will probably not be available for Home Guard units.

136

(C) Wiring Drill.
(i.) General:
(a) Men will work in pairs, every man doing his own work and no one else's, and working in the order laid down in the following drills. Men not working must lie down, and parties should keep five to ten yards apart.

(b) Materials must be dumped near the head of the work, in a regular order so that every man knows where to find what he wants.

(c) The line of the pickets must be marked out with tape, or the working party will lose direction. Tape may also be used to mark the route from the dump to the work.

(d) Work may be from either end. Men should work facing the enemy.

(ii.)
(a) Before learning the drill for a double apron fence, men must learn how to put in pickets, and how to fasten the wire.

(b) Pickets are laid out with their points in the direction of the enemy, at the exact points that they are to be put in. In driving in wooden pickets, the tops of the pickets, not the heads of the mauls, should be muffled, if muffling is necessary. Short wooden anchorage pickets are driven so that they are at right angles to the pull.

(c) To fix the horizontal wire to a wooden picket, pull the wire tight with the hand furthest from the head of the task. With the other hand pull a loop of the running end round the picket and windlass it to the standing part of the wire (see the diagram).

(d) To fix the diagonal wires, leave the standing end slightly slack and pass the running end twice round the picket, so that when finished the two ends cross one another and may then be windlassed.

(f) All horizontal wires start and end at the anchorage pickets at the ends of the task, and all diagonal wires begin and end at the top of a long picket.

(g) Men work in pairs and return to the head of the work on the completion of one task, where they can see or be told their next task.

METHOD OF FIXING WIRE ON POSTS

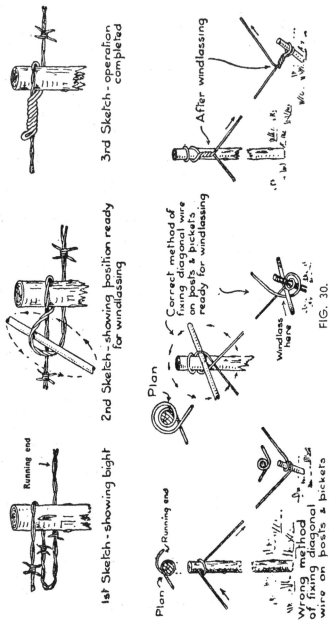

Running end

1st Sketch - showing bight

2nd Sketch - showing position ready for windlassing

3rd Sketch - operation completed

Plan

Correct method of fixing diagonal wire on posts & pickets ready for windlassing

Windlass here

Plan

Running end

Wrong method of fixing diagonal wire on posts & pickets

After windlassing

FIG. 30.

138

(h) If two numbers are shown running out wire, one carries the drum, the other makes the knots.

(i) The man carrying the coil should hold it so that the wire runs out from underneath.

(j) A lot of time is saved if the free end of the wire in a coil has a rag or tape tied to it, so that it can be easily found.

(k) Wire used for practice can easily be straightened by stretching, and hammering the kinks out with wooden hammers.

(iii.) Double Apron Fence with Wooden Pickets.

NOTE.—Iron screw pickets are not likely to be available in any quantity.

(a) **Party:** One commander and 10 men.

Stores:		Man-loads.
20 long wood pickets	....	5
40 short wood pickets	....	5
9 (65yd.) coils barbed wire	....	9
2 (130yd.) coils barbed wire for (diagonals)	....	4
4 mauls or sledge hammers	....	1
Total	....	24

Tools: 10 windlassing sticks.
1 pair cutting pliers.

(b) **First Duty:** Carrying stores.
Nos. 1 to 10 make two journeys out. N.C.O. directs. No. 3 takes out mauls or hammers on his second journey.
Nos. 7 to 10 (inclusive) make third journey and bring up remaining stores.

(c) **Second Duty:** Pickets (see Section C (ii.) b, p. 137).
N.C.O. paces 7ft. 6ins. intervals for pickets. Nos. 1 and 2 lay out pickets.
Nos. 3 and 4 drive in 8 long pickets.
Nos. 5 and 6 drive in 12 long pickets.
No. 8 lays out 16 short pickets (one at head of work and 15 along the front 6ft. from the fence and opposite the intervals. No. 7 begins driving them in, and is then helped by No. 8.
No. 10 lays out 24 short pickets (19 along the rear, and 6ft. from the fence, one at far end, and

139

four along the front). No. 9 drives them in
and is helped by No. 10.

(d) **Third Duty:** Wire.

Nos. 1, 2, 3 and 4, front diagonal wire (Nos. 1 and 3
run out wire, No. 2 fixes wire to long pickets,
and No. 4 to short pickets).

Nos. 5 and 6, bottom wire on front apron.

Nos. 7 and 8, centre wire on front apron.

Nos. 9 and 10, top wire on front apron.

Nos. 1 and 2, bottom wire on fence.

Nos. 3 and 4, second wire on fence.

Nos. 5 and 6, top wire on fence.

Nos. 7, 8, 9 and 10, rear diagonal wire. (Nos. 7
and 9 run out wire, No. 8 fixes wire to long
pickets, No. 10 to short.)

Nos. 1 and 2, top wire on rear apron.

Nos. 3 and 4, centre wire on rear apron.

Nos. 5 and 6, bottom wire on rear apron.

(iv.) **Barbed Wire Concertinas.**

(a) To make a concertina, draw a circle 4ft. in diameter.
Drive in nine wooden pickets at equal distances
round this circle, leaving 5ft. of the picket above
ground.

(b) No. 1 now gets inside the ring of pickets with
binding wire (thin wire cut into 4in. lengths).

(c) Nos. 2 and 3 run out the wires as follows:—Take
two complete turns round the circle of pickets and
at the foot of the posts with No. 12 plain wire, or
four turns with No. 14. Bind these wires at each
interval between the posts. This forms a strong
coil with which to pull out the concertina.

(d) Fasten the end of the barbed wire to the end of
the plain wire and take 24 turns round the posts
in a spiral form, keeping time with No. 1, inside
fixing with binding wire.

(e) No. 1, starting at the bottom and working round
and round, binds the wire to the turn below at
every **second** interval between pickets. As there
is an odd number of intervals the result will be
that the wire is tied first to the turn below and

140

then to the turn above, then below, then above, and
so on. Finish, as you began, with a ring of plain
wire.

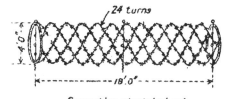

Concertina stretched out

*Concertina made up in
the standard way.*

FIG. 31.

(f) When the coil (130yds.) is finished, slip a lath
between the pickets and under the bottom of the
coil, and another over the top of the coil. No. I
holds the top down while Nos. 2 and 3 work the
coil up the pickets until it closes to a depth of a
few inches. The laths are tied with string, lifted
off the pickets and carried away.

(g) Concertinas can be carried by one or two men by
means of the laths. They are opened by cutting
the string, taking hold of the plain wire rings and
pulling out to 18ft.

(h) They should be pegged to the ground at intervals,
and may be stiffened by being dropped over
pickets three yards apart and windlassed to a wire
run along the heads of the pickets.

(v.) **Loose wire** for throwing between belts of concertinas or
apron fences to make the obstacle more effective is
prepared as follows:—

(a) Drive in two 6ft. pickets 3ft. apart and at right
angles to these at 1ft. 6in. apart, drive in two more.
Wind a coil of barbed wire round the four pickets
as though making a small concertina. Press the
turns together, and, tie in four places with string.
It is then ready for carrying on the shoulder.

(b) To use the wire so prepared, cut the string, carry
the spiral on the left arm, and walk along throwing
two or three turns at a time into the entanglement
with the right hand or a windlass stick.

(c) Another way of throwing loose wire is to uncoil
50yds. on the ground, cut it off, pick it up with a

141

long forked stick, twist it to and fro, and throw it into the entanglement, pressing it well down, and windlassing it here and there to the standing wire.

(D) ROAD BLOCKS.

(i.) **General:** These may be either absolute obstacles or temporary obstructions. The latter are intended to check armoured fighting vehicles, and to cause some of their crews to leave the cover of the vehicles. Such blocks must therefore be covered by the fire of the defenders.

Suspicious marks which suggest the presence of mines, and other dummies are useful for the same purpose.

(ii.) **Siting:** Blocks should be in positions which crews of approaching vehicles cannot see from any great distance. Otherwise they may be able to avoid them by turning off the road. Round corners, especially when the road is bordered by a steep bank, deep and broad ditch, high embankment, etc., are ideal positions. A block on a road with no lateral obstruction is useless. The A.F.V.'s will simply go off the road, round the obstacle, and back on to the road.

(iii.) **Construction:**

(a) Farm carts, etc., filled with stones or heavy material form good road blocks. Farm implements lashed or chained together will also be effective.

(b) **Trees,** especially big pines, felled across a road will stop all but big tanks. To fell a tree in a required direction, cut into it as far as the centre on the side on which it is required to fall. Then strain it in that direction by means of a wire or rope, and finish off with a cut four inches higher up on the opposite side. It will be all the more effective if the trunk is left attached to the stump.

(c) **"V" Trenches:** A V-shaped trench cut across the road 1ft. 6ins. broad and 2ft. deep, especially if covered with canvas or sacking on which dust or shingle is sprinkled, will stop fast-moving armoured cars. It is not suitable if the road is likely to be required for our own use.

(d) **Wire:** One or more belts of tangled wire form a useful obstacle against armoured cars. It can be placed in position quickly. It should be well pegged

142

down if possible, and well covered by small-arms fire to prevent removal.

(e) **Gaps:** It will sometimes be desirable that blocks should not close a road completely. In this case they should be made of two overlapping portions.

(f) **Tank Obstacles:**

(i.) Mines are only of use where the tanks must pass along a narrow track between tank-proof obstacles.

(ii.) Given time, particular localities, strong points, etc., may be protected against tanks by digging trenches with one wall vertical, six feet deep, the bottom slanted up gradually to make the other wall, so that from ground level to the vertical wall is about 15ft. The vertical wall, which is on the defender's side of the trench, can be strengthened with concrete, railway lines or sleepers, etc.

(g) **Fords** can be made difficult for infantry by throwing loose wire into them.

5—Explosives.

It is considered that certain engineer platoons within the battalion should be trained in the use of explosives, so that the battalion can carry out minor demolitions. Remember that major demolitions cannot be carried out without definite orders from Army.

As it is impossible to teach the use of explosives in a page or two, the following notes are for the guidance of instructors. An instructor with a sound knowledge of the subject should be appointed.

(A) EXPLOSIVES AND ACCESSORIES.

(i.) **Theory of Explosives: Explosion**—a sudden change from solid to gas, with resultant tremendous expansion. Rate of expansion varies, and results in **cutting, lifting,** and **shattering** charges.

Burning—a slow change from solid to gas.

Detonation—a practically instantaneous change.

(ii.) **Equilibrium of Explosives:** High-explosives are designed to be safe. Most of them are unaffected by knocking, or even applying a match to them. The service high-explosives are very safe. The commercial explosives are not so safe. Modern high-explosive requires a sharp shock to get them working—a detonator.

(iii.) **The Detonator:** This consists of a small quantity of unstable, unsafe, high-velocity explosive encased in a tube. Must be treated **with utmost care.** Keep detonators away from H.E. Sufficient strength to blow your fingers off.

    (a) **Detonators for use with Fuses:**
        Service No. 8 detonator.
        Commercial detonator.

    (b) **Electric detonator:**
        Service type.
        Commercial types.

    (c) Special detonators for use with depth charges, etc.

(iv.) **Primers:** A small cylinder of dry gun cotton, for use with the very stable service explosives such as damp gun cotton, ammonal. Service explosives must be very safe so that a bullet passing through them does not explode them; they therefore require a primer to detonate them.

(v.) **Fuses:** Fuse—detonator—(primer)—high-explosive. There are two types of fuse:—

    (a) **Burning:** Safety fuse, which burns at rate of 2ft. per minute (always test new fuse). Instantaneous fuse, which burns at about 100ft. per second. As these are affected by damp, always cut off the first six inches.

    (b) **Detonating:** F.I.D. and Cordtex.

Burning fuses can be set alight by means of a match or by a percussion cap, and will set off a detonator if placed in contact with the explosive of a detonator.

Detonating fuses are really thin tubes of H.E. and therefore require a detonator to set them off. They will then, on their own, detonate the H.E. Used to detonate several charges at once. Tie Cordtex round each charge, and lead back to the main lead. Join the shorter leads to the main lead by laying alongside and binding with adhesive plaster.

Be sure there are no sharp bends in the fuse. Now prepare a length of safety fuse with a detonator, and bind detonator to the end of the Cordtex with adhesive plaster. The safety fuse ignites the detonator, which then detonates the Cordtex.

(B) HIGH-EXPLOSIVES AND THEIR USES.

(i.) **Slab Type:** In 1lb. slabs. Requires a primer to detonate. Not sensitive to rifle bullet. Not affected by damp, but if soaked, will not detonate. Used as a **cutting explosive.** Types are:—

Guncotton, white slabs 6ins. by 3ins. by $1\frac{1}{4}$ins. (1lb.)
T.N.T., yellow brittle slabs (1lb.)

(ii.) **Powder Type:** Of consistency of sand. Requires primer to detonate. Attracts moisture, which makes it insensitive—no good. Not sensitive to rifle bullet. Packed in tins or waterproof packets of 4ozs. Best as a lifting or pushing explosive. Types are:—

Ammonal, grey powder, reacts chemically with copper, so keep away from copper.
Picric Acid, yellow powder, reacts chemically with lead, so keep away from lead.

(iii.) **Cartridge Type:** In 4oz. (sometimes 2oz.) cartridges wrapped in waxed paper or in cellophane. Usually have two rates of detonation. In order to obtain the higher rate of detonation for "cutting" charges, a primer should be used. Otherwise a detonator alone is sufficient. All (except P.E.) are sensitive to a rifle bullet. Not damaged by damp, but become most sensitive and dangerous after a month or two of damp conditions. Untreated types freeze at moderately high temperatures, when they become very dangerous. Most commercial types are treated so as not to freeze until very low temperature. Types are:—

(a) **Polar Gelignite:** A buff, cloudy jelly. Becomes dangerous if exposed to direct rays of sun or hot temperature. Causes headache if handled. Becomes more sensitive and dangerous after being in the damp for some time, when it becomes greasy. Common commercial explosive in New Zealand. Treated so as not to freeze at low temperatures.

145

(b) **Blasting Gelignite:** A buff clear, jelly. Freezes at 38 degrees F., when it becomes dangerous. Dangerous if exposed to heat, or sun rays. Causes headache if handled. Best blasting explosive.

(c) **Dynamite:** Red-brown plastic substance. Very dangerous if freezes or becomes hot. Not in general use nowadays. Also causes headache.

(d) **Eruptite:** A recent addition to commercial explosives. Occurs in bags 6ins. by $\frac{7}{8}$in. (potassium perchlorate). Bags are dipped in a special "oil" for three seconds before use. After dipping it remains potent for 24 hours.

(e) **Plastic Explosive:** A modern military explosive. Plastic substance, made in all colours, but usually yellow. Just like plasticine. Safe at all temperatures. Not sensitive to rifle bullets. Best all-round explosive. Very powerful. Does not give a headache. Mainly used for "cutting" charges. Supplies very limited.

(C) FIXING AND FIRING A CHARGE.

(i.) **Lighting Safety Fuse:** Damp is liable to penetrate safety fuse, so cut off the first six inches. Cut slantwise. Place match-head on safety fuse and strike box down against head of match, not across it. Test speed of burning.

(ii.) **Fix Fuse to Detonator:** Handle detonator very carefully; do not drop or bend. Measure with piece of grass. Insert square end of fuse into detonator carefully, but firmly. Do not force or twist. Crimp with pliers. Cover joint with adhesive tape if it is likely to be in the damp for a time. Carry in handkerchief, etc.

(iii.) **Insert Detonator into Primer or H.E.:** Do not force or twist. See that it will not slip out. Tie if necessary. Right and wrong angle at which to insert detonator into H.E.

(iv.) **Firing a Charge:** Safety fuse burns at rate of two feet per minute. If in doubt, test it. Connect fuse to detonator first, then insert detonator in charge. After seeing that all is secure, light the safety fuse and depart.

(v.) **Firing a Charge Electrically:** An electric detonator (distinguished by its two leads) is connected to the requisite lengths of wire, and fired by means of a car battery, torch battery, etc. If this trial detonator explodes, then replace with another electric detonator and insert into the charge of explosive, and fire as before. The current required depends on the circuit, and there are complicated ways of calculating it. For Home Guard purposes it is easier to actually fire a detonator as a trial. If this one detonates, the odds are that the next one will also.

(D) **SAFETY PRECAUTIONS.**

(a) **Detonators:** Keep them separate from other explosives, and know where they are. Handle firmly but carefully. Keep separate from main charge until last possible minute.

(b) **Fuse:** Is not dangerous when not connected by detonator to the charge. Do not try to light instantaneous fuse with a match. Treat F.I.D. and Cordtex as H.E.

(c) **H.E.:** Store underground if possible. Store away from detonators. Give them air. Keep incendiaries well away from explosives. **Do not cut with a knife. Do not smoke when using explosives.**

(E) **SUMMARY OF SEQUENCE OF OPERATIONS for Laying a Charge.**

(i.) **Beforehand:**
(a) Decide on size of charge.
(b) Inspect explosives.
(c) Prepare charge, in portable units if possible.
(d) Test fuse.

(ii.) **Beforehand or at Objective:**
(a) Prepare length of fuse (one end square, one end slanting).
(b) Insert square end of fuse into detonator.
(c) Crimp detonator on to fuse.
(d) Place primer in charge and tie in.

(iii.) **At the Objective:**
(a) Lay the charge.
(b) Place detonator with fuse into primer or charge.

(c) Strike matchbox against match held against slanting end of fuse.

(d) Retire.

(iv.) **Remember:**

    (a) Keep detonators separate.

    (b) Do not use metal instruments on explosive.

(v.) **Personal Stores Required:**

    (a) Matches.

    (b) Jacknife and pliers.

    (c) String.

    (d) Torch.

    (e) Watch.

(F) DEMOLITIONS.

(i.) The main use of demolitions from the point of view of the Home Guard is to delay the enemy by the destruction of communications over which he must pass, or material which will fall into his hands. Bear in mind that the execution of a few complete demolitions at points in communications where there is no alternative route will delay the enemy more than a number of demolitions each of which can be easily repaired or circumvented. The possibility of effecting destruction by means other than explosives should not be overlooked. This is especially important where available explosive is limited. Wooden bridges, etc., and stores may be burnt. Trees are usually more quickly felled with an axe.

(ii.) Avoid concrete structures. Culverts under roads are easy to blow. Girder and wooden bridges may be attacked. It is possible to block roads with rocks, or blow away part of the road. Rails are easy to attack.

(iii.) Two types of charges:—

    (a) **Cutting Charge:** The quick detonation cuts right through metal or masonry. The explosive must be hard up against the object to be cut, with no air cushion between. If it is not possible to do this, fill up the space between with clay. Best to press the explosive well into the object to be cut.

DEMOLITION OF RAILWAYS.

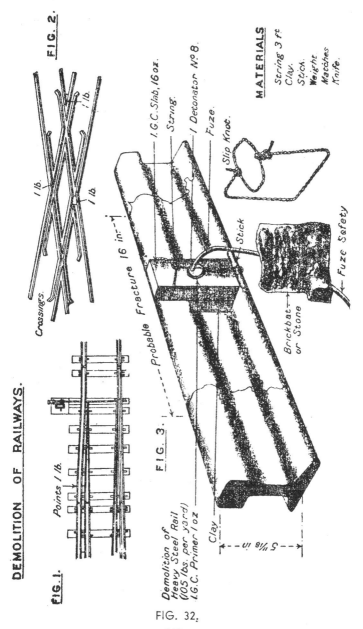

FIG. 1.

Points 1 lb.

FIG. 2.

Crossings.

1 lb.

1 lb.

1 lb.

1 lb.

FIG. 3.

Probable Fracture 16 in.

Demolition of
Heavy Steel Rail
(105 lbs. per yard)
I.G.C. Primer 1 oz.

I.G.C. Slab, 16 oz.

String.

1 Detonator No. 8.

Fuze.

Slip Knot.

Stick.

Brickbat
or Stone.

Fuze Safety.

Clay.

5 11/18 in.

MATERIALS

String 3 ft.
Clay.
Stick.
Weight.
Matches.
Knife.

FIG. 32.

149

DEMOLITION OF RAILWAYS.

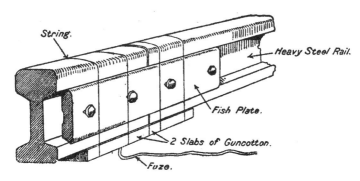

FIG. 33.

(b) **Mined Charge:** Best use a slower explosive (blasting). The expansion blows out the earth, etc. Used under roads or railways, and behind the abutments of bridges, etc.

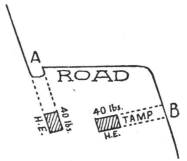

FIG 34.—DEMOLITION OF A ROAD.

(iv.) The weight of explosive to be used in various demolitions can be calculated from the following formulae:—

Material.	Lbs.	Remarks.
Hardwoods	$3D^3$	D = Diameter in feet.
Softwoods	$\frac{2}{3}D^3$	B = Breadth in feet.
Iron or Steel	$\frac{3}{2}Bt^2$	T = Thickness in feet.
Masonry	$\frac{1}{2}BT^2$	t = Thickness in inches.

(v.) Place the charge up against anything you want to cut, or inside and tamped for a mined charge. The diagrams show the best positions for charges in various types of works.

(vi.) Remember, bridges must not be destroyed except on orders from the Army.

CHAPTER IX.

Signalling and Messages.

1—Messages. 2—Means of Communication. 3—Signalling Drill.
4—Field Signalling.

1—Messages.

Accuracy and speed are the two essentials in transmitting messages and, in order to attain them, certain rules of procedure are necessary, both to assist signallers and to ensure uniformity of method throughout the signal system.

The following is a list of miscellaneous signals used to facilitate the rapid and accurate transmission of messages by V/T, L/T and W/T:—

A.—General answer on semaphore.

AA.—i: Unknown station call sign. ii: All after.

A̅A̅A̅.—Break signal before plain language text.

A̅ᴋ.—End of transmission.

B.—Have you received message?

CK.—Figure check to follow.

F.—Make no further signals.

ii.—Separative signal (used between groups of figures to make the division clear).

iii.—Full stop written thus ⊙

I̅M̅I̅.—Send again.

K.—Go on.

LL.—Your signals are too strong.

MH.—Move higher or further away.

ML.—Move to your left as you face me.

MM.—Signal preceding the numerator of a fraction.

MO.—Move lower or closer.

MR.—Move to your right as you face me.

NA.—I can make no further signals.

OL.—Open light.

Q.—Wait.

R.—Received correctly.

SR.—"Send replies" method.

ST.—"Normal" (straight through) method.

T.—General answer on Morse.

$\overline{UK}$.—Block letters.

V.—From.

$\overline{VE}$.—The commencing signal. "I have a message for you."

W.—Your signals are too weak.

WA.—Word after.

WB.—Word before.

$\overline{XE}$.—Fractional bar.

Eight dots.—The erase signal.

In some cases a signal is represented by two or three letters with a bar placed above them. This bar indicates that the letters will be run together when signalled by Morse without any pause between them, e.g., $\overline{AR}$ will be sent as .—.—.

The following additional signals, known as priority prefixes, denote the degree of priority of a message, and are included in Offer. They must be written in the Call and Instructions space by signaller, when he finds such priority ordered.

OiiU.—Most immediate.

OiiA.—Emergency air attack.

O.—Emergency operations.

P.—Immediate.

D.—Important.

Types of Messages.

The Written Message.—This is a message written on a message form, a record of which may be required to be kept. It will contain an "address to" and an "address from"; the "reference line" should have been completed and the "time of origin" inserted by the originator.

The $\overline{VE}$ Message.—This is a message which may be given verbally to the signallers to transmit, or which may be written down, simply as a text, without the addresses or references required in the "written message."

The use of $\overline{VE}$ messages should be of great value to a commander in action. especially if his signalling terminals are close to him, enabling him to ask a question quickly and get an answer quickly, and to convey, quickly, tactical or administrative orders or information.

Message as dealt with by Originator.

I. Address To and From.—Units will be designated by their code names. If the message is intended for the H.Q. of a unit, no other designation will be used other than the code name of the unit, e.g., Salo means O.C. Salo or Adjutant Salo.

2. The Reference Line—

    (a) The originator's number. This is filled in by the originator for reference purposes and consists of letters and figures.

    (b) The date. Only the figures representing the day of the month will be written, e.g., 29th May is written 29.

    (c) In reply to number—. This space contains the originator's number of the message to which reference is being made. Its use renders such remarks as "reference your . . ." in the text unnecessary.

3. The Text—

    (a) The text may consist of plain language, cipher or code.

    (b) Cipher is written in groups of five letters or figures and is essentially a secret representation of plain language.

    (c) Code may consist of pronounceable words, invented for the purpose of representing sentences of plain language.

    (d) Block capitals are to be used for (i.) place names, (ii.) personal names, (iii.) regimental names, (iv.) code words for units, (v.) the word "not."

    (e) The four cardinal points of the compass are to be written in full, the intermediate points as initials, e.g., north, east, S.W., N.N.E.

    (f) Roads are indicated by the names of places on them, and these follow the word "road," e.g., Road NAPIER CLIVE HASTINGS.

    (g) Where possible give map-references for places.

    (h) Describe positions from right to left, looking towards the enemy, from rear to front in an advance, and from front to rear in a withdrawal.

    (i) Indelible pencil must not be used.

4. Signature. The originator signs his name and rank only, in one of the two signature spaces, thereby giving his instructions regarding the use of cipher.

5. Originator's instructions. Degree of priority. If the originator is allotting any degree of priority to a message, or any instructions such as "to await arrival," he will write it in this space.

6. Time of origin (T.O.O.). This is the time at which the originator signs the message, and is filled in by him. The 24-hour clock code is used, and at all times will simply be a four-figure group, e.g.:

>0530 is 5.30 a.m.
>1005 is 10.5 a.m.
>1245 is 12.45 p.m.
>1918 is 7.18 p.m.

The Message Form as dealt with by Signal Personnel.

(a) Serial number. This is a reference number used in the signal register.

(b) The date stamp. The call of the station, followed by date in the form 19/6/41, should be written here, to meet Home Guard requirements.

(c) Call and instructions. The latter only will be represented by correct procedure signals here, e.g., P. ICW.

(d) Number of groups. In this space is filled in the figure denoting the number of groups in the message. ˙

(e) Rules for counting the number of groups. A word of plain language, a collection of letters in cipher, a code name or a series of figures is counted as one group, e.g.,

>ACCOMMODATION
>CQLRZ
>ODON (code name).
>1049

(f) Any combination of letters, figures or signs (except the hyphen) that obviously has one meaning in itself is counted as one group, e.g.—

>N.C.O.
>B/5.

(g) Full stop is counted as one group.

(h) A pair of brackets or of inverted commas is counted as one group, e.g., (hut) or "hut" is counted as two groups.

(i) Time handed in. The signaller will at once write here time the message is passed to him (24-hour system).

(j) Operator's spaces. Only the left one for **In** messages or the centre one for **Out** messages will be used.

The block signal $\overline{UK}$ is not counted at all.

The Text.—The signal clerk or signaller may not alter the text of a message in any way unless instructed to alter names of units into code names.

T.O.O. (time of origin), T.H.I. (time handed in), T.O.R. (time of receipt).

Additional miscellaneous signals required for "written message procedure":—

AAA.—Break signal used immediately before the originator's number in a plain language written message.

BT.—Break signal used—
   (i.) At the end of the text in all written messages.
   (ii.) Immediately before the originator's number in a cipher message.

C.—Correct.

DU.—Hyphen.

FI.—Decimal point.

G.—This message must be repeated back.

GR.—Signal preceding the figures which denote the number of groups in a written message.

ii.—Separative signal.

ICW.—If liable to fall into enemy hands, the message must be in cipher.

KK.—Brackets.

RR.—Inverted commas.

T.—Signal to show that a written message is for retransmission. It then immediately follows the VE.

W.—Used as the signal for the word "repeated" if it appears in the "address to" space of a written message. It is then preceded and followed by a separative, thus, iiWii, sent as one group.

XE.—Oblique stroke.

Z.—(i.) Signal to show that a written message is for delivery. It then immediately follows the VE.
   (ii.) Used in the "address to" of a written message to signify that the following is the address or list of addresses to which the message is addressed for action. It is then preceded and followed by a separative thus, iiZii, sent as one group.

If a message is to be sent to two or more addresses for action at BOTH, the offer is VE ZiiT.* The 'Addresses To" will be preceded by iiZii.

If the message is to be sent to two or more addresses for action at ONE, but for information at the others, the offer is

156

VE ZiiT*. but the "Addresses To" will be preceded thus:—iiZii
LIVE iiWii HOME PAKI.

As clarity is essential, the originator must write "Repeated"
before addresses to which the message is sent for information
only. Omission of this word would indicate that all stations
addressed should act upon the message.

*NOTE.—The "T" will, of course, only be used if retrans-
mission is actually necessitated.

Use of Separative Signal ii—

(1) It is sent as part of the priority prefixes OiiU and OiiA.

(2) It is sent between the parts of, and at the end of, the
Reference Line.

(3) It is sent between the Time of Origin and the Time
Handed In.

(4) It is sent between any two groups where a figure ends
the first and another begins the second, e.g., 408 5-lb.
bags.

(5) It **may**, at discretion, be sent anywhere in the transmission of a message, when the operator considers it
advisable for ensuring that the receiver will count up
correctly. For example, on either side of a doubtful
group; BLACKBIRD is so often thought of as one group
that if it were essential to send it as BLACK BIRD, it
should go as ii BLACK ii BIRD ii.

(6).It is used in the signals iiZii and iiWii, one of which
precedes the "Address To" in "Written Messages" (see
above).

2—Means of Intercommunication and Their Characteristics.

The means of intercommunication fall under four headings:—

(i.) Line telegraphy and telephony (L/T).

(ii.) Wireless communication, including wireless telegraphy
(W/T) and radio telephony (R/T).

(iii.) Visual telegraphy (V/T).

(iv.) Message-carrying agencies.

These methods have varied characteristics which suit different
conditions. In principle it is unsound to rely entirely on one
means of intercommunication, and therefore (iii.) and (iv.) will be

dealt with under this heading; headings (i.) and (ii.) being omitted because of their importance for more advanced and fully equipped training units.

1. The chief advantages of V/T are that the apparatus is simple and portable. V/T provides a method of intercommunication which is quick to establish and therefore valuable during mobile operations for short messages.

Its disadvantages are that it is a slow method compared with L/T; stations must be able to see one another; therefore dust, smoke, bad weather and battle conditions tend to make V/T slow and unreliable. It may be seen and read by the enemy and thus disclose the position of headquarters, and give away information.

As all methods of V/T are comparatively slow, it is essential that signallers should be trained to a high standard not only of signalling, but of alertness, observation and speed in establishing communication.

2. The instruments used are:—Flag, Lamp, Heliograph and Shutter.

(i.) Semaphore provides a useful method of sending short messages over short distances.

(ii.) Morse signalling by flag in the forward area is very likely to attract hostile attention and must therefore be used with the greatest discretion; its visibility and handiness make it extremely useful to attract attention and establish communication quickly. The Morse flag may prove of great value for the transmission of short messages.

(iii.) The lamp, short range or long range, is the principal visual instrument in the field. It is comparatively easy to conceal and the personnel operating it can do so under cover.

(iv.) The heliograph, being dependent on the sun, requires conditions such as are prevalent in the Middle East and in eastern and tropical theatres.

(v.) The shutter is useful for Morse signalling over short distances in the forward area.

3. The standard rates for reading and sending are:—

Buzzer	....	....	....	10 words a minute
Semaphore		....	....	10 words a minute
Lamp and heliograph		....	8 words a minute
Flag	....	....	....	6 words a minute

4. As has been stated, accuracy in sending is the very foundation of good signalling. Nowhere is this more essential than in visual telegraphy. Failure to have due regard to it will result in many requests for corrections, with consequent loss of time. It is far better to send slowly until the efficiency of the reader has been gauged. Remember that he may be a novice—not his fault—or that he may be operating under conditions more unfavourable than you can suspect.

5. Let all flag sending, morse and semaphore, be clear and crisp. If you find you must send slowly, do not unnecessarily slow the PARTS of a morse LETTER; rather lengthen the pauses between LETTERS, with a further lengthening between GROUPS.

6. If you ARE good, (a) you are only as fast as your reader, and (b) all the more reason why you should help him.

7. Finally, your motto must be: "Get the message correctly sent to its destination as speedily as circumstances allow."

3—Signalling Drill.

(A) The names used for the letters in flag training, and for verbal spelling when required to avoid mistakes, are:—

AC	JOHNNIE	SUGAR
BEER	KING	TOC
CHARLIE	LONDON	UNCLE
DON	MONKEY	VIC
EDWARD	NUTS	WILLIAM
FREDDIE	ORANGE	X-RAY
GEORGE	PIP	YORKER
HARRY	QUEEN	ZEBRA
INK	ROBERT	

In visual telegraphy the letters underlined above will always be thus named. The others should only be used to avoid any ambiguity, and when it is necessary to spell over a telephone.

(B) Morse Flag Drill.

The following are drill orders for opening out a squad to the necessary intervals for flag drill. Instructors should reduce to a minimum the time spent on these drill movements so as not to shorten the instructional period.

Movements are carried out in the same manner as in infantry drill, the position of the flag at "attention" and "stand at ease" being that of the rifle.

During movement the flag is carried at the "short trail."

(a) The squad falls in in two ranks and is numbered.

(b) **"TO THE LEFT TO TWO PACES EXTEND."** Men turn left and march out. Turn to front, taking time from last man.

(c) **"REAR RANK TWO PACES STEP BACK—MARCH."**

(d) **"ODD NUMBERS OF THE FRONT RANK FOUR PACES FORWARD, EVEN NUMBERS OF THE REAR RANK FOUR PACES STEP BACK—MARCH."**

(e) **"RE-FORM RANKS—DOUBLE."**

(f) **"DISMISS."** When an officer is present, the squad, after turning to the right, will pass the flag to the left hand, holding it at the short trail, salute, and break off.

(C) I. Flag Drill by Numbers—After Opening the Ranks.

NOTE.—After the ranks have been opened, the squad may be turned or inclined in any direction so as to have the wind at its back.

"PREPARE TO SIGNAL. SQUAD—ONE."

Carry the pole across the body with the right hand and grasp it with the left hand just above the right, gather in the flag with the left hand, which should be opposite the left breast.

"SQUAD—TWO."

Carry the left foot about 12 inches to the left, at the same time slide the right hand down the pole, grasping it about half-way between the butt and the flag, the right arm to hang easily at its full extent, the pole to point upwards and across the point of the left shoulder. The flag to be clear of the body.

"SQUAD—READY."

Letting the flag fly, raise the pole with the right hand, grasping it at the extremity of the butt with the left hand, which should be level with the chin and about eight inches from it; both elbows to be free from the body and turned slightly downwards, the eyes to look to the front, the pole to be at the same angle as at the "prepare to signal" position.

Prepare to signal from the ready—

"PREPARE TO—SIGNAL."

Lower the pole with the right hand, at the same time gather in the flag with the left by pulling the pole through it, the right arm to hang easily at its full extent, the left hand opposite the left breast, the pole to point upwards and across the point of the left shoulder.

"ORDER FLAGS BY NUMBERS. SQUAD—ONE."

Slide the right hand up the pole, grasping it just below the left hand, the flag to be gathered in.

"SQUAD—TWO."

Bring the flag to the "order," at the same time bring the left foot in to the right and the left hand smartly to the side.

2. Morse Training Method (Flags):—

(i.) General:

(a) Stand, according to the wind, directly facing the distant station, or with the back to it.

(b) Keep flag unfurled (simplified if tip is made to describe a slight figure of eight).

(c) Keep good time, and do not take flag too far for either dot or dash. Make a sharp check and pause at every "dash position."

(d) Never pause at the "Ready" until the signal (i.e., letter, figure, or barred group) is completed.

(e) Do not grip flag too tightly, and let the left hand work the flag, while the right acts as a pivot.

(f) Adopt the "Ready" and "Prepare to Signal" positions briskly, and avoid all forms of lackadaisical sending.

(ii.) Dots and dashes should first be taught by numbers, and then in quick time.

DOT BY NUMBERS—ONE: Carry flag smartly from READY to corresponding position on opposite side of body (i.e., to "Position of the Dot"). **TWO:** Return flag smartly to READY.

DOT IN QUICK TIME—GO: Combine ONE and TWO above as a continuous movement, with no pause.

SUCCESSION OF DOTS, OR THREE, ETC., DOTS—GO: Make required number of dots with no pauses at all until completed.

DASH BY NUMBERS—ONE: Take flag smartly from READY to opposite side of body until flag pole is inclined just below the horizontal. Stop it sharply. This is "Position of the Dash." **TWO:** Return flag briskly to READY.

DASH IN QUICK TIME—GO: Combine ONE and TWO above, but observe a distinct pause at Position of Dash.

SUCCESSION OF DASHES: Make the succession, with distinct pause at Position of Dash, but none at the Ready.

When this has been learnt, letters and figures should then be made. Words of command should be given at the Prepare to Signal; squad, taking time from front, comes to Ready, pauses, sends signal, pauses, returns to Prepare to Signal.

Short words may then be sent. After each letter, return to READY. When word is completed, return to PREPARE TO SIGNAL. This is the accepted indication of the end of a group, and must be distinct between words of a message.

(D) Semaphore Flag Drill.

1. Fall in. **"FALL—IN."**
   The squad will fall in in two ranks, dressing by the right, arms close to the sides and at the full extent, flags held perpendicularly, one in each hand. The poles will be grasped six inches from the butts, the flags being gathered in between the first and second fingers of each hand. This is the "Prepare to Signal" position.

2. Stand at ease from the "Prepare to Signal." **"STAND AT—EASE."**
   Cross the right pole over the left pole about three inches from the extremity of the butts, elbows slightly bent resting easily on the hips; at the same time carry the left foot about twelve inches to the left.

3. Attention from the "Stand at Ease." **"SQUAD—ATTENTION."**
   The left foot will be brought in to the right and the flags to the "Prepare to Signal."

3a. The **"READY"** from the "Prepare to Signal" or from the "Stand at Ease." Flags are lowered in front of legs at full extent of arms; right pole is crossed over left about three inches from tips. Forefingers extend along poles. Butts are pressed firmly against forearms. Left foot is carried about twelve inches to left, if not already there in the "Stand at Ease" position.

4. The drill for opening and re-forming ranks is the same as for morse flag drill, the flags being carried during movement, in the "Prepare to Signal" position.

5. Examples of commands to be used in semaphore training:—
   (i) **LETTER AC SQUAD—ONE** (squad makes letter) **TWO** (flag down to ready).
   (ii.) **LETTER AC, TAKING THE TIME FROM THE FRONT, SQUAD—GO.**

(iii.) **LETTERS AC TO GEORGE, TAKING THE TIME FROM THE FRONT, SQUAD—GO** (i.e., the squad goes through the first circle).

6. Notes on method (semaphore):—

(i.) Throughout training each man should name aloud the letter he is signalling.

(ii.) At first a demonstrator should show the letters when facing the same direction as the squad.

(iii.) Later, the instructor or an N.C.O. should face the squad, and form the same letter as the squad, so that the men learn to associate the sending and receiving forms from the beginning.

(iv.) An N.C.O. or senior private should be detailed to stand in front of the squad, where all can see him, to give the time.

(v.) Letters and other signals are indicated by relative positions of one or both arms and the body. As it is POSITION, and not DURATION OF TIME, that distinguishes letters, particular care must be paid to the correct angles of the arms, or signals will be misread. The alphabet, and other signals, should be learnt in circles:—

1st circle: A to G. Right arm makes A to D; left E to G.

2nd circle: H to N, omitting J. Right arm remains at A; left travels successively from B to G.

3rd circle: O to S. Right arm remains at B; left travels from C to G.

4th circle: T, U, Y, Erase. Right arm remains at C; left travels from D to G.

5th circle: Numerical J, (or alphabetical) V. Right arm remains at D; left travels from E to G.

6th circle: W and X. Right arm remains at E; left travels from F to G.

7th circle: Z. Right arm at F; left at G.

(vi.) GENERAL: The flags should be regarded as an extension of the arms, therefore flag and arm should be in the same straight line. Assist this by pointing forefingers along pole, and letting butts be pressed firmly against the forearms.

Keep flags in plane of the body; do not let flags cover one another.

Turn on hips whenever an arm crosses the body, otherwise arm or flag will not project far enough outwards for easy reading at any but the shortest distances.

Within a group, flags are not brought back to the READY, but are moved sharply to the positions for the next letter. Return to READY at end of a group.

Exception: If a letter is to be repeated, as in "RALLY," the first "L" is made, flags are brought quickly to READY, and without pause, put out again to "L."

After initial stages, if one flag is already in position for the next letter, keep it steady, as in AN.

In such successions as HO, both arms may be moved through 45 degrees, or the one at B may be kept steady while the other moves from A to C.

(vii.) In practising letters "by numbers," ONE will indicate that class moves flags to the letter position; TWO will bring them back to the READY.

In "quick time," bring flags to position ordered, make a short pause, and return to the READY.

Always face the distant station squarely, irrespective of wind direction.

4—Field Signalling.

TYPES OF VISUAL STATIONS AND GENERAL DUTIES OF PERSONNEL IN CHARGE.

1. The visual stations established at two places between which communication is required are known as "terminal stations."

2. When two visual stations cannot communicate direct with each other owing to ground conditions or distances, one or more retransmitting stations are established at selected intermediate points.

3. The N.C.O. or signaller placed in charge of a visual station will pay particular attention to the following:—

   (i.) That, on arrival near the point at which the station is to be established, personnel and stores of the station are left under cover while he makes a reconnaissance and selects the actual site.

(ii.) That visual station discipline is rigidly enforced.

(iii.) That, while work is proceeding, there is no unnecessary talking or moving about.

(iv.) That efforts to attract the attention of a distant station are continuous until replied to.

(v.) That no unauthorised person is allowed to loiter within hearing of the station.

(vi.) That, when his station moves more than a very short distance, all stations with which it is in communication are warned beforehand; the direction in which it is moving and the approximate point and time at which it will again call up being indicated when possible.

(vii.) That, when work is temporarily suspended, the direction of each distant station is either noted by reference to some conspicuous landmark or by aligning two or three pickets or stones. The latter precaution should always be taken if a station is closed during daylight and is likely to be again required at night.

(viii.) That, if there is any likelihood of messages, etc., falling into enemy's hands, they should be destroyed.

4   At a terminal station there are three sets of duties in sending a message and three in receiving one.

In sending the duties are:—

(i.) Calling.

(ii.) Sending.

(iii.) Reading answers.

In receiving the duties are:—

(i.) Reading.

(ii.) Writing.

(iii.) Answering.

The detailed duties of station personnel are as under:—

TRANSMITTING.

CALLER:

(1) Caller is in charge.

(2) Writes down a VE message, if given him verbally.

(3) Has charge of order of messages. Despatches them in order of priority or T.H.I.

(4) Dictates groups to sender.

(5) Spells long, unfamiliar, or ambiguous words.

(6) Repeats or spells when sender asks him.

(7) Gives necessary orders to sender when receiver wants "repeats."

(8) Orders re-signals if unanswered.

(9) Is responsible for correct sending, and filling in of details on message form.

SENDER:

(1) Attends to his instrument and regular sending.

(2) Sends just what CALLER tells him.

(3) Applies to CALLER if in doubt of spelling, etc.

(4) Requests stronger or weaker signals, if required.

ANSWER READER:

(1) Continuously watches distant station and reads out each letter as sent by it.

(2) Calls "GROUP" when distant flag is lowered, or light obscured.

(3) Asks for stronger or weaker signals, if required.

RECEIVING.

WRITER:

(1) Writer is in charge.

(2) Writes down any $\overline{VE}$ messages, for reference, and to ensure correct delivery.

(3) Enters on message form just what reader calls.

(4) Says on hearing "Group," YES.

(5) Orders sending of "R" when satisfied.

(6) Orders sending of any signals to obtain corrections.

(7) Is responsible for correct reception, and filling in of necessary details on message form.

READER:

(1) Watches distant station continuously. Calls out letter by letter what they send.

(2) Calls "Group" when he sees it.

(3) Asks for stronger or weaker signals, if required.

ANSWERER:

(1) Sends answers as ordered by WRITER.

(2) Sends request for stronger or weaker signals.

(3) Sends signals as ordered by WRITER to obtain corrections.

ORDERLIES OR RUNNERS.

Such a system should be complementary to a signal service, and to be efficient should, like the latter, consist of trained personnel.

While simple, quick for long messages over short distances, permitting of carriage of maps and sketches, and providing secrecy, it has the possibilities that an orderly may lose his way, become exhausted or a casualty, or become captured along with his message.

Such contingencies must receive due consideration before messages are entrusted to this service.

Orderlies must receive clear, definite instructions concerning routes, with which latter they should endeavour to familiarize themselves beforehand. Messages should be carried where they can easily be found. Receipts for messages delivered must be obtained, and a report made quickly if message cannot, despite all efforts, be delivered.

Orderlies should be under the charge of a signal N.C.O., who should use them in strict rotation. They should be close to the signal office when on duty, and must rest when off duty.

They should, in daylight, acquaint themselves with the location of all H.Q.'s they are likely to be sent to, especially after moves have been made.

They should receive some instruction in elementary map-reading, and should be men of good intelligence who possess plenty of initiative and power of observation.

CHAPTER X.

Elementary Tactics.

1—Battle Procedure. 2—Sentries. 3—Scouts. 4—Patrols.
5—Defence. 6—Protection on the Move. 7—The Attack.
8—Ambush. 9—Street Fighting.

While it is impossible to cover the subject of tactics in one short chapter, the following sections on the various operations of war should be of use to leaders of the Home Guard as a guide to further study and practical work.

The company commander must devote special attention to the training of his section commanders in grasping situations rapidly, issuing orders clearly and quickly, and adopting suitable dispositions for the task in hand. The intelligent application of tactical principles must therefore be so ingrained and developed that once the roles of their sections have been explained to them, they can carry on without further orders from their platoon commander.

1—Battle Procedure.

(i.) Time is a vital factor in battle and every endeavour must be made to shorten the period of reconnaissance and preparation, once operations have commenced. Men who are harassed and hurried lose much in morale.   Commanders should exercise intelligent anticipation, use warning orders, do everything to avoid delays, and issue orders in a cool, decided, and unhurried manner.

(ii.) In most operations much time can be saved by intelligent planning before the company commander sets out on his reconnaissance. The period from receipt of orders by the company commander till the forward sections go into action may be divided into three stages:—

Stage I: (a) Company commander issues warning order, and commences his reconnaissance.

(b) Platoon commanders with runners move to rendezvous at which company commander will

> meet them and give his orders (in view of
> ground, if possible).
>
> (c) C.S.M. or company second in command marches
> company up to prearranged point.

Stage 2: (a) Reconnaissance by platoon commander, who
first sends back a runner with orders to platoon
sergeant to march platoon forward, and instruct
section commanders to meet him at a specified
point.

> (b) Platoon sergeant moves platoon forward to
> a forward area.
>
> (c) Company H.Q. is opened.

Stage 3: (a) Section commanders carry out quick reconnaissance and return to their sections.

> (b) Section commanders issue orders and move
> their sections.
>
> (c) Platoon H.Q. is opened.

(iii.) In making a reconnaissance an officer will take the following steps:—

(a) Ensure he has all available information regarding
situation.

(b) Be clear as to the object of his reconnaissance.

(c) Consider what he is going to look for.

(d) Before starting, study map, pick out likely viewpoints,
routes, etc.

(e) Consider time available.

(f) Then make mental plan for the reconnaissance, including
routes and time-table.

(g) Before setting out, leave information so that he may be
found if urgently required.

On orders received from his superior, and as a result of his
reconnaissance, he is now in a position to prepare his plan.

2—Sentries.

(A) (i.) The security of a post depends on the care with which
sentries are posted, and on their alertness and efficiency.

(ii.) Sentries must be posted so that they can warn the
section silently, by day or night. They must remain in
the post and avoid any unnecessary movement. During

darkness, sentries should be posted in pairs, and the pair should be in touch with each other and able to communicate without movement. The position of reliefs should be so arranged that they can be awakened for their tour of duty without disturbing the rest of the section.

(B) Sentries must understand the following procedure for dealing with persons approaching the post:—

(i.) If anyone approaches, the sentry will immediately warn the post.

(ii.) If the person or party approaches close to the post the whole section should be ready to fire. The sentry will call out "Halt" just loud enough to be heard, and not until it is quite certain that the party can be shot if the order is disobeyed.

(iii.) If the order to halt is obeyed, the section commander will order the person or commander of the party to advance and give an account of himself; the remainder of the section covering the party with their weapons.

(iv.) If the order to halt is not obeyed immediately, fire will be opened by the whole section without hesitation. On very dark nights, when the party must be allowed to approach to within a few yards of the post before being challenged, it is usually better to rely on the bayonet.

(C) All sentries must know:—

(i.) The direction of the enemy.

(ii.) The extent of the ground they have to watch.

(iii.) The position of the section posts on their right and left.

(iv.) The names of any landmarks to their front.

(v.) The procedure to be followed if they see anyone approaching the post.

(vi.) Particulars of any friendly patrols due to return through their post.

(vii.) The signal for defensive fire.

(viii.) The password.

(D) **Guards Mounted on Buildings, etc.**

(i.) When guards are mounted on buildings, bridges, petrol stations, etc., for protection, duties will be carried out with no ceremony. Sentries will not be tied down to a fixed beat, but will be mounted behind cover, or will "snoop" round, using cover. If they stand in the open, or move on a regular beat, enemy scouts can easily locate them, and later stalk and destroy them. Posts will be selected with a view to the sentry's protection. If sentries are posted in a position where the post cannot be covered by the fire of the remainder of the section, then they will be posted in pairs, so that one may cover while the other examines anyone approaching the post.

(ii.) If a sentry is to be posted in an isolated spot, three or four men under an N.C.O. should be posted and the post prepared for all-round defence.

(iii.) In challenging, a sentry will not disclose his position, but will cover the person with his rifle and order, "Halt. Hands up," and then, "Guard—Stand to." When the guard have the person covered, he will be questioned or examined.

3—Scouts.

(i.) Scouts are used to prevent a section being surprised, and for reconnaissance. When a platoon is deployed the section commander is responsible for his own protection, especially on an exposed flank.

Scouts work in pairs. They move forward in bounds from one objective to another. When the objective of one bound has been selected, one of the pair chooses his route to it, and moves forward as rapidly as possible, while the other remains in observation, and covers the first with fire if necessary, until he is signalled up. If the first man gets into difficulties the second can inform the section commander, in time for him to take action. Scouts should see without being seen, and use their rifles only in self-defence. Their aim is to locate enemy strong points and weapon sites, so that these can be either attacked separately or avoided and isolated.

(ii.) Scouts can be used by reserve sections to report on the position of forward units. When scouts have information for the section commander one man should remain in observation, while the other goes back to report.

4—Patrols.

There are three types of patrols:—
- (a) Reconnoitring patrols.
- (b) Fighting patrols.
- (c) Standing patrols.

(A) RECONNOITRING PATROLS.

(i.) **Reconnoitring Patrols** may be sent out on either—
- (a) Reconnaissance for purposes of protection to give warning of the presence of the enemy, e.g., sent out from outposts before dawn to discover if the enemy have worked up close to positions during the night.
- (b) Special reconnaissance, as for example, gaining information about enemy defences, reconnoitring lines of advance, etc.

Strength, usually one section.

(ii.) **Orders:** The success of a patrol depends on the leader. Before going out he will receive orders including:—
- (a) What is known of the enemy.
- (b) Position of forward detachments of our own troops.
- (c) The object of the patrol (straightforward questions to be asked: "Is there any enemy in HALL FARM?")
- (d) When patrol is to go out, and when return.
- (e) Route to be followed.
- (f) Password.
- (g) Whether bodies of our own troops have been notified that patrol is going out.

(iii.) **Preparations** before setting out:—
- (a) Reconnaissance: Leader should study the ground, noting landmarks and aids to keeping direction at night, bounds, obstacles, observation points. He will then make his plan.
- (b) He will see that every man knows the orders so that if he becomes a casualty the patrol can carry on.
- (c) Patrol to go out lightly equipped: rifles and few extra rounds only.
- (d) Patrol to move silently at night, see equipment does not rattle.
- (e) No letters, papers, maps to be taken on patrol.

(iv.) **The Route:** This is decided by the officer who sends the patrol out, but it is a general route only. The patrol leader must carefully plan his exact route. Do not use the same route twice.

(v.) **The approach** to an objective is to be planned by the patrol leader. He is to get information without fighting. It is better to approach from the rear or a flank. Do not do the obvious. Advance will usually be by bounds from cover to cover. Make provision for protection against surprise, and method of getting information back if the patrol is wiped out. This may be done by the use of scouts and get-away men.

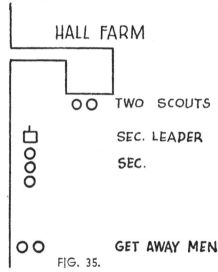

HALL FARM

TWO SCOUTS

SEC. LEADER

SEC.

GET AWAY MEN

FIG. 35.

The distances between scouts, patrol and get-away men will depend on the ground and visibility. Must always keep patrol in view.

(vi.) **Withdrawing** the patrol will still be by bounds, a portion of patrol withdrawing to next position in rear **from which they can cover the withdrawal of the** remainder of the patrol.

(vii.) **By night,** it is best not to move by bounds, but at a steady pace with frequent halts. Silence is essential. If a surprise collision with enemy takes place, it is best to go straight in before he has time to collect

his wits. Keep to low ground by night, use shadow as
much as possible.

In all circumstances patrol leaders will use their initiative and
modify any of the above to suit existing conditions.

(B) FIGHTING PATROLS.

(i.) Fighting patrols are usually at least one platoon sent
out under an officer. They carry full equipment and
weapons, and are sent out to act as covering parties
in defence, to delay the enemy during a withdrawal, to
harass the enemy, or to secure identifications. They
must be prepared to act offensively.

(ii.) **Formations** adopted should be such as will give maximum protection to front and flanks. When not in close
contact with the enemy, and moving along a road, the
patrol may have a point section forward, with scouts to
watch either flank. If in closer contact with the enemy,
a more open formation must be adopted. The position
of the patrol commander to be where he can best
command his patrol (usually well forward). Distances
between sections will depend on the ground.

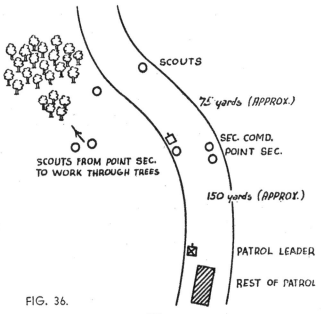

SCOUTS

75 yards (APPROX.)

SCOUTS FROM POINT SEC.
TO WORK THROUGH TREES

SEC. COMD.
POINT SEC.

150 yards (APPROX.)

PATROL LEADER

REST OF PATROL

FIG. 36.

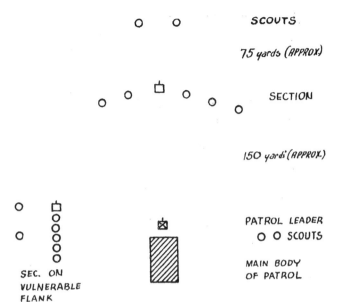

SCOUTS

7.5 yards (APPROX)

SECTION

150 yards (APPROX.)

PATROL LEADER
O O SCOUTS

MAIN BODY
OF PATROL

SEC. ON
VULNERABLE
FLANK

(iii.) **Advancing:** When enemy is encountered, patrol advances by bounds from feature to feature. The leader selects a position, and the forward section advances to it under cover of fire (if necessary) from the remainder of the patrol. On gaining the position, this section then covers the advance of the remainder of the patrol to the position. Positions selected should have a good field of fire. In approaching a building, bridge, etc., thought to be occupied, it should be well covered by the patrol while scouts advance to investigate.

(iv.) **Withdrawing** will be on similar lines, i.e., bounds from position to position.

(v.) **By night** the best formation to adopt will depend on the darkness of the night, distance from the enemy, nature of the ground, etc. Usually patrols will have to move in closer formation than by day. Advance by short bounds of about 30 yards, with frequent stops for listening. In night operations of this sort it will seldom be possible to attack with covering fire from a flank; actions will be more in the nature of shock action.

STANDING PATROLS.

    (i.) Standing patrols are sent out to watch an approach by which the enemy are expected to advance, usually such places as bridges, road junctions, etc., and give early warning of enemy approach. They may be ordered to change position or withdraw if forced to do so by the enemy.

    (ii.) The strength of a standing patrol depends on its task, and what resistance it is expected to offer. The strength must be sufficient to provide the requisite number of reliefs for sentry duty.

    (iii.) The patrol leader must know:—
        (a) Points he is to watch or hold.
        (b) His route out and back.
        (c) What he is to do if enemy appears.
        (d) How often to report and by what means.
        (e) Any signals he is to give on seeing enemy.
        (f) How he is to be recognised on approaching his own lines.
        (g) Length of time post to be occupied.

    (iv.) The patrol is entirely responsible for its own protection, therefore all-round protection is important. Select a position with no covered approaches the enemy may use. Have a good line of withdrawal, and a long field of fire to prevent the enemy getting too close. Scouts to watch both front and flanks. Select a position which is not obvious.

5—Defence.

(A)   (i.) The **object** of defence is to defeat the enemy attack by fire.

    (ii.) The **principles of defensive action** are:—
        (a) Defensive position, however strong, is useless if defenders have not the will to defend and the skill to make full use of their weapons.
        (b) Object to inflict maximum casualties on enemy with least loss to selves.
        (c) Defence in depth is essential.
        (d) Only one degree of resistance—last man and last round, unless otherwise ordered.

(iii.) **Modern methods** of attack are based on the principle of infiltration. A defensive area consists of a series of posts. After a preliminary bombardment a number of these posts will be out of action, and these comprise the weak spots of the defence. An attack by a large number of small groups of the enemy will find these soft spots, and by neglecting the strong points of the defence, and wriggling small parties through these soft spots, deep penetration by small parties is achieved, and the enemy is then in a position to attack headquarters, supplies, communications, bridges, etc., thus paralysing the whole defence. Later, parties of the enemy will endeavour to widen the small gaps in the defence by attacking strong points from the rear or flanks. Just as such an attack depends on the initiative and leadership of corporals and sergeants for its success, so is successful defence dependent on the leadership of section commanders.

(B) (i.) **Selection of defensive position:** The following points must be kept in mind (see also Chap. VIII., Sec. 2):—

(a) Surprise is important.

(b) Tank obstacles to be made full use of.

(c) Observation over approach of enemy is important.

(d) Series of defended localities, mutually supporting, sited in depth to prevent penetration.

(ii.) Surprise is rather difficult to achieve in defence, but every effort must be made to obtain it. Concealment by the use of all available cover and camouflage is important. Silent posts to draw the enemy. Small arms fire in defence depends almost entirely on concealment and surprise. The enemy should be kept completely in the dark as to the defender's location and dispositions— he should never be able to divine what he is up against. Obvious trenches are useless. They must be dug to ensure maximum concealment, and there must be alternative positions. The more difficult it is to obtain concealment, the more important it is to prepare alternative positions to force the enemy to dissipate his fire. Sections to change from one alternative position to another, and every means taken to deceive the enemy as to the actual position occupied. Every care must be taken to reduce tracks to a minimum, as they are easily visible from the air.

(iii.) Tank obstacles are of utmost importance in defence. Our main tank obstacle is the sea, and the enemy will endeavour to form a bridgehead on our shores. He must be attacked before he can be reinforced or establish himself. Resource must be shown and mobility utilised until he feels that every hedge conceals an ambush and every road a trap. In this country the enemy would be restricted largely to the roads, so road defence must be organised in depth, and full use made of improvised traps. Railway cuttings, river lines, steep embankments, and stop-banks may all be useful tank obstacles. The enemy will probably use tanks to give supporting fire to his infantry, in the earlier stages, owing to the difficulty experienced by naval craft engaging shore targets (some ships, however, have guns fitted for shore work in which charges are reduced).

(iv.) Observation of the enemy is important at all times. During the hours of darkness patrols must be sent out frequently. Coast watching stations must be established in the precautionary period.

(v.) Defended localities: The defence consists of a series of localities organised in considerable depth, for all-round defence, and sited to afford each other mutual support. Localities to be strengthened by artificial means, such as wire, mines, obvious cover on beaches mined, etc. Localities to be provisioned and supplied with water, ammunition, etc., to enable the post to hold out and make it evident that they intend to if outflanked or surrounded. If infiltration takes place and they hold their ground, they prevent the gaps being widened and the attack loses impetus and fails. Posts must realise that by so holding out they make the enemy very much more vulnerable to the counter-attack when it takes place. Rear platoons of forward companies must be so sited that they can bring fire to bear on the front, and also they must be prepared to counter-attack if required. Reserve companies and reserve platoons of forward companies must have prepared plans for counter-attacks on important positions should these fall into enemy hands. Reconnaissance and plans to be made as far in advance as possible, and the attacks to be rehearsed. In beach defence, arrange for Road Blocking Posts at road junctions to stop enemy moving inland with vehicles along roads.

(C) (i.) **Conduct of the Defence:** The degree of resistance to be offered by forward troops must be very clearly laid down by higher command, also the authority to order their withdrawal. The enemy is likely to attempt the formation of bridgeheads at numerous points, and should he succeed, the opportunity may occur to launch a vigorous counter-attack. The most successful type of defence is aggressive defence. The period of waiting in prepared positions is dangerous to morale and discipline, and commanders must do their utmost to inculcate the aggressive spirit. Aggressive defence includes active and organised sniping, fighting patrols, counter-attacks. Infiltration to be met with a sharp counter-attack, making use of ground, covered approaches, and fieldcraft to isolate and destroy the enemy. The deliberate giving of ground may offer an opportunity for a successful attack. Isolation of advanced units by road destruction.

(ii.) **Counter-Attack:** A rapid counter-attack has a great disorganising effect upon an enemy. Commanders must therefore be prepared to launch immediate counter-attacks, and to this end will study the ground, make plans, and rehearse as early as possible.

(D) (i.) **Action of Platoon Commander.**

Preliminary: Having been allotted his locality by his company commander, he makes a reconnaissance of the area to decide where to locate his section posts (see also Chapter VIII.):

(a) Section posts must be mutually supporting, sufficiently close for control, sufficiently far apart to avoid being vulnerable target for artillery.

(b) Mutual fire support with flank platoons.

(c) All-round defence in event of being over-run.

(d) Best use of natural cover for concealing trenches. In open country, mislead enemy by digging extra trenches.

(e) Patrolling of dead ground.

(f) Plan of wiring, obstacles, etc. (all under fire of platoon).

179

(g) Adequate supply of ammunition, grenades, etc.

(h) Sanitation.

Orders: Information, enemy, strength, where contact likely, when. Own troops: On either flank and rear. Obstacles.

Intention: "In the event of an attack, hold this position, etc."

Method: Allocate ground to section commanders. Position of section posts. Organise duties and work of sections. Orders re time available for digging, wiring, blocks, etc. Sentries to be posted by day, by night. Equipment on at night. Restriction of all movement in forward zone. S.O.S. Defences to be manned one hour before dawn, and one hour after sunset. Patrols. Sanitation. Position of platoon H.Q. Synchronize watches.

Notes: Platoon commander will frequently visit section posts by night and see that they are alert. He is accompanied by a runner.

In addition to above, platoon commanders of reserve platoons will prepare plans for counter-attacks.

Remember enfilade fire (from a flank) is much more effective than frontal fire.

(ii.) **Section Commander's Responsibilities** are:—

(a) To see that his section's weapons are placed so that they can fire on the ground allotted to them.

(b) See that the section is properly dug in and concealed (see Chap. VIII).

(c) See that a proper routine is observed.

(iii.) **Section Commander's Action.**

(a) **Preliminary Action:** After receiving his orders from his platoon commander, he will assemble section in concealed position in rear. Posts sentry to watch for hostile aircraft, and messages from platoon H.Q. Reconnoitres site of post with an eye to the ground.

(b) **Verbal Orders:** Before digging commences:—Give general situation, (i.) enemy, where he is, line of approach, time; (ii.) own troops, sections in rear, and flanks, platoon H.Q. Any outside support. Task of section, when fire to be opened. Digging. Names of prominent landmarks. No lights or smoking in forward localities. Time to stand-to at dawn and dusk. S.O.S. Password. Sanitation.

(c) **Further Action:** While his section is digging:—
Make out a range card. Work out sentry roster for
night (double sentries). See he has plenty of
ammunition. Night arrangements (equipment on).
Men study ground in front for possible night work.
Rehearse cut-and-dried plan for defence of post by
night. Inform re patrols out. Fix time for inspection of rifles, ammunition, emergency rations, etc.,
night and morning. Inform that no man can leave
post without permission.

(iv.) **Instructions to Sentries:** Security of the post
depends on the alertness and efficiency of sentries,
and the care with which they have been posted.
In giving orders to a sentry it is best to start from
the front and work in clockwise direction:—

Front: Direction of enemy, extent of ground to
watch, landmarks, any patrols out and when
returning.

Right: Name of section on right, landmarks, etc.

Rear: Position of platoon H.Q., section in rear.

Left: Section on left, names of landmarks, etc.

At post: S.O.S., password, action if anyone
approaches the post (arrange for another to
cover person while sentry inspects papers,
etc. Sentry careful not to mask line of fire).
Alert at all times; warn section commander
if anything unusual seen.

(E) **Gas in Defence:** The enemy may use non-persistent or persistent gases:—

(a) Non-persistent gas such as tear or lethal gas requires
suitable weather conditions, and its use is improbable.
It requires careful preparation, and is dependent on
stable meteorological conditions with a steady following
wind. Any change in wind may catch the attacker at a
greater disadvantage than the defender. Again, this type
is of little use against widely dispersed troops, for to be
effective the vapour must assail persons in a highly concentrated and steady stream. The gas is dissipated
quickly. This would entail a tremendous expenditure of
gas for a very small effect, apart altogether from considerations of methods of liberation.

(b) Blister (mustard) gas is a persistent gas and remains in a locality for several hours or days, depending on weather conditions. It is not likely to be put down as a heavy concentration on areas over which the enemy hopes to advance. It has been stated that spray from aircraft will have little effect if the aircraft can be kept at 2000 feet or more by means of small arms fire. Gas spray is most effective against columns and massed troops, but of little use against dispersed troops.

(F) **Dive Bombing** is very effective against untrained troops by reason of the terror it causes. Recent experience has shown that, although dive bombing has considerable moral effect against inexperienced troops ,the casualties inflicted are surprisingly small. Small arms fire is effective. Troops must not engage targets at too great a height, however, as this will give their positions away. Men in trenches suffer very few casualties from this form of attack. It is most effective against roads blocked with troops or refugees.

(G) Defence is never automatic. Think of new ways of deceiving the enemy, keep him guessing as to your dispositions and intentions. Remember, a few well-aimed bursts of fire will do much more damage to men huddled in boats than twice the fire against the same men after they have landed and deployed, but his landing craft may be protected against small arms fire by means of armour plate.

6—Protection on the Move.

A commander who succeeds in surprising his opponent gains a moral advantage that helps considerably to counter-balance superior resources which the enemy may possess. To guard against surprise the commander puts out protective detachments, which may be:—

> Advanced guards.
> Flank guards.
> Rear guards.

(A) ADVANCED GUARDS.

(i.) The commander of a force advancing towards the enemy will detail such advanced guards as are necessary. The duties of an advanced guard are:—

(a) To reconnoitre.

(b) Brush aside enemy detachments and deny him the opportunity of gaining information, and also to avoid delay to the main body by small parties of enemy.

(c) On meeting opposition it cannot overcome, to seize ground and hold enemy while commander of the main force makes his plan and puts it into execution.

(ii.) An advanced guard will usually consist of one-quarter to one-third of the troops.

(iii.) The advanced guard is responsible for its own protection, so its commander details one-quarter to one-third of the guard to act as protective troops to the main guard. These protective troops are known as the vanguard, and they in turn guard against surprise by sending forward smaller detachments. The distances between these bodies of troops will depend on the ground; the distances given in the diagram below are approximate only and will vary greatly in different circumstances.

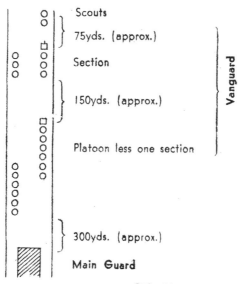

FIG. 38.

(iv.) On encountering the enemy the advanced guard commander must act with boldness and vigour. A
commander can usually take rather more risk in an
advanced guard attack than normally.

(v.) Orders to the advanced guard commander will include:
  (a) What is known of the enemy.
  (b) Strength of the advanced guard.
  (c) Intentions of force commander, including objectives
  to be gained during advance.
  (d) Hour at which main body will start, and route to
  be followed.

(B) **FLANK GUARDS.**

(i.) If there is a possibility of an attack from the flank, the
commander will detail flank guards, who will move parallel
to the main force either on roads or cross-country.

(ii.) These flank guards will usually move by bounds from
tactical feature to tactical feature. They will put out
scouts, make their own reconnaissance, and keep contact
with the main body. They will pay particular attention
to lateral roads.

(C) **REAR GUARDS.**

(i.) A withdrawal is carried out when a commander wishes
to avoid or postpone a decision by battle, or after an
unsuccessful action. If pursuit is not close a rear guard
proper is the procedure, i.e., an "advanced guard
reversed." If pursuit is close, successive positions are
occupied by either the same or different bodies of men.

(ii.) Withdrawals are usually carried out according to a
timed programme, so that the enemy may be held up
on a certain line to give the main body time to prepare
a defensive position. Another reason for timing is to
co-ordinate the action of several rear guards.

(iii.) The **method of timing** is usually as follows:—
  (a) Time laid down up to which position is to be
  denied the enemy.
  (b) Time laid down at which forward positions will be
  finally evacuated by rear parties.
  (c) Time at which rear parties will cross a given line
  in rear of the position (to enable artillery to put
  down fire forward of this line after the time
  specified).

(iv.) **Essentials** of a rearguard action are:—
  (a) An intact front; you must not allow any enemy

penetration, for where troops are moving backwards this is far more serious.

(b) Keep enemy in ignorance that you are withdrawing. Thin out over a period, maintaining fire to make him think you are still there.

(c) Thin out along the whole front simultaneously.

(v.) The **object** is to impose delay on the enemy and allow main body to withdraw unmolested. To do this, make the enemy deploy to attack successive positions—attacking to strike thin air, and then having to close again to continue the pursuit.

To do this, make him deploy far enough away to enable you to have time to get out without being committed to a real fight. This is done by selecting good fire positions with a long field of fire, and occupying these with sufficient fire to make him deploy and attack, then by selecting positions with a good getaway, get out before he can attack.

In a rearguard position a wide front will be necessary because of unprotected flanks; this will mean little depth to the defence. Put all your weapons forward. In other words, go in for "window dressing." Concealment is of the utmost importance: the enemy must not know what you are doing; he must not know your weakness.

(vi.) **Getting Away:** Platoon assembly positions are formed to which men go as soon as they leave forward posts. When platoons are complete they are led to company assembly positions (note, the rear party may go direct to company assembly position).

All positions and routes to them are to be thoroughly reconnoitred, and guides will lead the men back.

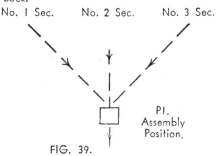

No. 1 Sec.   No. 2 Sec.   No. 3 Sec.

Pl. Assembly Position.

FIG. 39.

185

Before withdrawal of troops commences, there must be some troops in the next position to be held.

(vii.) If very hard pressed, a counter-attack with **very limited** objectives may be necessary. Temporary cessation of fire and then a sudden burst may surprise the enemy and impose caution. There must be no running fight. Men cannot run and fight too. Always have some troops in the next position to be held.

(viii.) **Action of Company Commander** in the withdrawal:—

(a) On receipt of verbal orders, take down in writing:
Intention.
Time up to which forward defended localities to be denied enemy.
Time to start thinning out.

(b) Orders will include:—
Information: Enemy; own troops.
Intention.
Method: Detail platoons to foremost defended localities.
Reserve platoons.
Time up to which foremost defended localities to be denied enemy.
Time thinning out to start.
Location of next position in rear.
Who to reconnoitre it.
Which platoons to occupy it.
Time to move to it.
Time for withdrawal of forward platoons.
Forward assembly position.
Demolitions and platoon tasks.

(ix.) **Action of Platoon Commander** in the withdrawal:—

(a) Having been given instructions by the company commander as to the method of withdrawal, he will—
Choose his platoon assembly position.
Reconnoitre best and most covered route to company assembly position and decide how he will move his platoon to it. Arrange for guides.

(b) Issue his orders:—
Information of enemy and own troops.
Intention.

Time up to which the foremost localities must be
denied the enemy.

Time thinning out is to commence.

Signal to indicate final withdrawal.

Point out platoon assembly position.

Location of company assembly position.

(c) Administration, etc.:—

Position of R.A.P. and company H.Q.

Synchronize watches.

Arrangements for feeding.

7—The Attack.

(A) (i.) The object of attack is to close with the enemy and
destroy him or drive him from his position.

(ii.) The principles are:—

(a) Plan must be simple, based on best information
available.

(b) Plan must be thoroughly understood by subordinates
who must carry it through with resolution.

(c) Every body of troops to be given a definite task.

(iii.) Audacity and surprise are irresistible, although before
advancing it will usually be necessary to neutralize the
enemy's fire. This may be achieved by—

(a) Use of ground to give cover from view and fire.

(b) Adoption of formations to reduce casualties.

(c) Covering fire to destroy or blind the enemy.

(iv.) Types of attack vary according to the ground and the
enemy's preparations. Where the enemy has not had
time to dig himself in, and where good covered
approaches exist, the platoon will be able to help itself
forward by the use of ground and fire. The section(s)
giving covering fire to be as far to the flank as possible.
By placing the section giving covering fire well to the
flank, the assault sections can advance much closer to
the enemy before masking the covering fire. If the
enemy has had time to erect wire and dig, heavier
supporting fire will usually be required to cover an

attack. Here the attack is carried out on a timed programme with machine-gun and artillery support. Probably the Home Guard will be required to carry out attacks of the first type only, adopting guerilla harassing tactics rather than attacks in force.

(B) (i.) The platoon commander will give his orders to his section commanders from a position giving a good view of the ground if possible. These orders will include:—

(a) Information of the enemy, position, strength, etc., and the position of friendly troops on right and left.

(b) His intention.

(c) The objective (pointed out on ground).

(d) Formation in which platoon will advance.

(e) Tasks of the sections (assault, supporting fire, etc.)

(f) Starting line and forming up position.

(g) Any change in equipment.

(h) Where walking wounded go.

(i) Position of platoon H.Q.

(j) Zero.

(ii.) The section commander will make a quick reconnaissance after he has received orders from his platoon commander, and will then return to his section. Having made his own plan, including route and formation in which section will move, he gives his orders to his section. They will include:—

(a) Features of ground pointed out and named.

(b) What is known of the enemy.*

(c) Position of friendly troops.

(d) Platoon objective, route, formation.

(e) Task of section.

(f) Route of section.

(g) Action to be taken on capture of objective.

(h) Where walking wounded go.

(i) Position of platoon H.Q.

(C) (i.) In the advance the section will make use of such cover as is available, varying the formation to suit the ground. If there is no way round exposed ground swept with enemy fire, the section will extend and rush across. Avoid bunching, cross obstacles quickly, and keep going at a steady pace until held up, then work forward.

(ii.) The aim is to advance as close to the enemy position as possible without undue loss, and without having to check the speed of the advance by opening fire. If advance becomes no longer possible, however, the whole platoon will push forward by the use of ground, fire, and manoeuvre. Having penetrated to close quarters, the position will be assaulted. The whole area must now be searched and trenches, dug-outs, houses, etc., cleared out. Grenades are very suitable for this purpose. Isolated machine-gun posts may be stalked by one or two men armed with grenades under cover of fire from the rest of the section.

(iii.) As soon as a position has been captured, send men forward to take up positions from which they can repel possible counter-attack. The period following the capture of a position is one of slight disorganisation when troops are very vulnerable to counter-attack, therefore all precautions must be taken. Send back a message to platoon headquarters. This process is called consolidation.

(iv.) Although a section consolidates on reaching an objective this does not usually end the attack. The success so gained must be exploited by pushing on while the enemy is on the run. This is usually done by fresh troops pushed through the original troops.

(D) **Night Attacks.**

(i.) It is very difficult for troops to advance in the face of machine-gun fire, and an attack by night may be much more successful and much less costly than one by day. There are certain difficulties in night operations, however. Control is difficult, the situation is more obscure by night, there is a liability of misdirection and confusion. These dangers may be overcome by training, discipline, and careful preparation, and a body of men so trained will often gain the moral and material benefits of a successful surprise. Night attacks have the advantages of avoiding the aimed fire of the enemy, of surprise, and of moral effect. Frequently a well-trained body of men can neutralize an overwhelming superiority of fire power possessed by an enemy by means of a well-planned night attack. The plan for a night attack must be simple.

(ii.) A night attack resolves itself into six stages:—
  (a) Reconnaissance and preparation.
  (b) March to assembly position.
  (c) Advance of assault troops from assembly position to forming-up place.
  (d) The assault.
  (e) Consolidation.
  (f) Exploitation.

(iii.) **Reconnaissance:** All should view the ground both by day and night, to select landmarks, suitable stars, etc. Objectives will be selected that are easily found at night. Preparations to be as complete as possible, and calculations of time and space worked out. The orders for the attack to be explained to all concerned beforehand. Everyone must know:
  (a) The object of the attack, the objectives, routes.
  (b) The formation to be adopted.
  (c) The part he has to play.
  (d) Action in case enemy is not surprised.

(iv.) At the **Assembly Position** platoon commanders will satisfy themselves that:—
  (a) Magazines are charged, but rifles not loaded.
  (b) Silence is preserved; no smoking, coughing, talking, etc.
  (c) Watches are synchronized.

(v.) Advance forward of assembly position will usually be in battle formation, the assembly position being selected so that it can be easily found at night. The distance between the assembly position and the objective will depend on the ground and the vigilance of the enemy. Routes forward to be reconnoitred and compass bearings taken. The advance should be preceded by a protective detachment. The advance will be continued steadily at the same pace. Troops should reach the forming-up place in time for a short halt before the assault. During this halt leaders should verify their positions and the line of advance.

(vi.) **Assault** formations are governed by the following:—
  (a) Distances depend on visibility and necessity for control. On dark nights manoeuvre is impossible and depth is not required. On bright nights some manoeuvre is possible and some depth is necessary to enable this manoeuvre to be carried out.

(b) Essence of success is surprise. Timings should be such that the attack strikes the enemy front everywhere at the same moment.

(c) First wave of the assault should be heavy, so that bulk of troops will be forward of enemy's defensive fire. All ranks to understand that once the forming-up place is left, the attack goes through whatever happens. Assault to be carried out in silence. No backward movement to be permitted. Success depends on swift, silent, resolute action, to surprise the enemy completely.

8—Ambush.

The success of an ambush depends on the care and thoroughness with which the leader makes his plans. Every effort must be made to ensure the utmost possible surprise. There are two types of ambush:—

      (a) Road ambush.

      (b) Rail ambush.

(A) ROAD AMBUSH.

(i.) **Information:** By means of scouts, etc., the leader will obtain as much information as possible of the enemy. He must know:—

How the enemy move (foot, horse, M.T.).

Strength of party in men and arms.

Number of vehicles (A.F.V.'s).

Time they pass.

Enemy formations, scouts, etc.

(ii.) **Planning:** Select a road which small parties of the enemy use, and a part of that road that is suitable for ambush, e.g., where it is narrow with banks. Obstacles may be erected, or even a harmless bottle of water standing on the road, or a square of paper will make the enemy stop to examine it. Select a place with a good line of advance and perhaps a better line of withdrawal; broken or wooded ground is suitable. The position must be inconspicuous and covered from air observation. Good fields of view and fire are essential. Give detailed orders as to procedure to be followed, and when fire is to be opened.

(iii.) **The Action:** Get into position secretly, and post sentries on high ground to warn of the enemy approach by means of prearranged signals. Do not be too eager, but let the action proceed according to plan. For example, the leader may arrange his ambush so as to have a small decoy force on one side of the road. When this force opens fire the enemy debus and make for the shelter of a bank, etc., on the opposite side of road from which they can bring fire to bear, and are protected from the decoy force. It is then time for the main party, which has been so placed as to enfilade this obvious cover, to open fire with automatic weapons. After the action the leader will secure all papers and maps, and will arrange for the removal of the wounded.

(iv.) **Withdrawal:** Withdraw by signal. Discipline is essential here, as there is a tendency for men to remain collecting souvenirs. No man must be captured.

(B) **RAIL AMBUSH.**

This is similar to road ambush, and the same procedure is to be followed except that it is to be combined with some method of derailing the train. The greater the speed of the train the greater the damage. The rear trucks being least affected, will require most attention. Derailing may be accomplished by loosening rails (especially on a bend), by cutting both rails (1lb. H.E. on each), or by 10lbs. H.E. buried under ballast (see Chap. VIII., Sec. 5).

9—Street Fighting.

Street fighting is a slow and exhausting process, the success of which depends on thoroughness. Usually undertaken by small bands of men (sections). When the section leaders have received their orders they make sure they understand them and know what action they are expected to take. They then pass orders on to their men, making sure each man knows his job. Impress on men discipline, no souvenirs. Any questions? Synchronize watches.

It is as well to number the section so that if leader becomes a casualty these numbers are the sequence of leadership. Success depends on pushing on, so section cannot stop to attend to casualties. Apply first field dressing and push on ,coming back to collect later. There are two types of street fighting:—

(a) Concealed street fighting.
(b) Open street fighting.

(A) CONCEALED STREET FIGHTING.

(i.) Here the enemy have possession of the buildings, and will be concealed in upper floors and on roofs. Tall buildings will be used as look-outs, so always approach under cover of darkness, and after a preliminary reconnaissance surround the town. Each section is given a certain portion of the town, and a rendezvous is established. All instructions are to be given well beforehand, and the best time to attack is at dawn.

(ii.) **Weapons:**

Rifle is of little use in street fighting, which is entirely short-range work. Its long barrel makes it a cumbersome weapon.

Grenades, either Mills or home-made, are an important weapon.

Pistol—an important weapon in street fighting.

Sub-machine-gun—best of all weapons for street fighting.

(iii.) **Methods:**

Formations depend on circumstances, but as a general rule section divides in two when advancing along the street, half on each side, hugging the buildings. In each half-section there will be one man in front detailed to watch windows and roofs of houses on opposite side of street for enemy. Similarly one man will follow each half-section to deal with anyone opening fire after the section has passed. Remember that back-yards are sometimes a better line of advance than streets.

Action if fired upon from one house: The half-section under fire crosses the street and advances to the house, when both half-sections attack. If both half-sections are fired upon from opposite houses, they both cross the street to the house from which they were fired on, and attack.

193

Houses to be entered as quickly as possible. A door may be opened by (a) grenade placed at bottom of door; (b) firing sub-machine-gun into lock; (c) ramming the door. If you fail, do not go back the way you came, as enemy will be waiting, but advance. On entering a house the leader quickly details men to various rooms. The enemy is probably on the upper floor, and has an advantage.

Rooms are each attacked by two men. Do not peep round the door, as this is what the enemy is waiting for. One man flings open the door and rushes in, so effecting surprise. The other man waits a moment, then also enters the room. After cleaning out the room, the men report back to their leader. When houses are adjoining it, it is sometimes possible to advance from house to house by blowing holes in dividing walls, and if the room is occupied, throw in a grenade before entering.

Cellars are important places which are difficult to attack. They are best attacked via the stairs rather than the grating. Four men, armed with grenades and pistols, stand at head of stairs, and on the signal all jump together, landing with their backs to each other. When the firing starts they may be reinforced. H.E. or smoke grenades are useful in attacking cellars.

(iv.) **Reorganisation:** After having cleaned out a house, the leader details men to search for weapons, ammunition, and men. Collection of souvenirs is discouraged. He makes central dump of weapons and ammunition, reorganises, and pushes on.

(B) OPEN STREET FIGHTING.

This occurs when the enemy have just taken the town, and have not had time to organise or occupy buildings. Both sides are in the open, and on the same footing. The method of attack is to advance in extended line, shooting during the advance. The main task is to push on, using buildings for covering fire if necessary. Control of the men is essential but difficult under these conditions.

(C) WHEN DEFENDING A HOUSE.

(i.) Avoid the roof, which may be a death trap and is easily seen from the air.

(ii.) Take all glass out of all windows. Experience has shown that glass splinters cause more casualties than bullets. Barricade windows with sand bags, etc., if there is time, otherwise with mattresses and pillows.

(iii.) A wet blanket hung in front of a window so that it sways gently will stop a bullet.

(iv.) Post sentries where they are protected, and from where they can see both up and down the road. Build a loophole in sandbags.

(v.) Carefully watch both front and back doors.

(vi.) Carry out a reconnaissance and decide on more than one line of withdrawal. Explain these to the men. Retire on the command of the leader only.

(vii.) If explosion occurs and party must quit the house, do not rush out. Make an orderly withdrawal via one of the lines of withdrawal.

(viii.) If possible, arrange for all entrances to be covered by fire from some other building.

(ix.) Doors not required should be securely barred and bolted (stout battens, steel rails, etc.)

(x.) Arrange good fields of fire.

(xi.) If possible, place obstacles such as wire close up to foot of exterior walls to prevent the placing of explosive close to walls and also to prevent sudden rushes.

(xii.) Illumination at night where possible.

(xiii.) Arrange for fire-fighting.

(xiv.) Arrange visual signalling, supply of water, S.A.A., etc.

CHAPTER XI.

Transport.

1—Constitution of Transport Section.

(A)   (i.) Home Guard Transport is:--
          (a) A light truck of the 15cwt. type to each platoon.
          (b) One two to three-ton truck per company.
          (c) Sufficient transport to shift the whole unit if possible, though this is considered unlikely to be needed.

     (ii.) Wherever possible, select vehicles for the Transport Section from private owners, and make it perfectly clear to them that in the event of an emergency the vehicle promised must be available to the Home Guard.

    (iii.) In connection with the personnel of the Transport Section, this should consist of men with a high standard of physical fitness, as, should their services be required, the work that would be expected of them would be of a very tiring nature.

    (iv.) Wherever the Home Guard unit is large enough.to require a Transport Section of approximately 30 men or more, the Transport Section will then form a platoon of H.Q. Company.

     (v.) Should the unit not be large enough to form its own platoon, attach it to a specialist platoon, which would also include the signallers, ambulance, etc.

(B) A few suggestions in connection with a parade of motor vehicles:—
     (i.) The time the parade is called for is the time that the vehicles are ready to move off.
    (ii.) Before going on parade, check the vehicle thoroughly— petrol, oil, water, lights, etc., tyres and body.

(iii.) Before commencing a journey, check the oil pressure, the steering, and the brakes.

(iv.) Eight vehicles make one unit under an N.C.O.

(v.) When vehicles are on parade, before moving off, the drivers will stand to their vehicles. That is to say, stand at ease beside their vehicles approximately one yard from the driver's door.

2—Signals.

Embus: Right forearm is moved up and down from the elbow several times, palm upwards.

Debus: Similar movement, palm downwards.

Start Up Motor: Circular motion of right forearm as though cranking car.

When the motor is started the driver extends his right arm smartly out from the cab. He does not bring it in until the N.C.O. acknowledges his signal by pointing to each man in turn.

The signal to advance is given by bringing the right arm forward, palm up at the back, down at the front (an under-arm movement). From the front bring the hand smartly back to the shoulder and down to the side.

Halt: Right arm extended straight above the shoulder.

Increase Speed: Double sign.

Decrease Speed: Same as debus.

Switch Off: Washout sign.

3—Movement of Troops by M.T.

(A) (i.) There are two types of movement:—

(a) **Tactical:** In forward areas when enemy is anticipated.

(b) **Strategical:** In rear areas where enemy action is not anticipated except from the air.

(ii.) **Factors Affecting Movement** are:—

(a) The normal average speed of vehicles concerned.

(b) The density of vehicles or v.t.m. (vehicles to the mile).

(c) Number of available routes between two given points.

(d) Nature of country to be traversed.

(a) Speed is reckoned in m.i.h., that is to say, "miles in hour," including stops, gradients, etc., over the given route. This is distinct from m.p.h. or "miles per hour."

(b) **Density,** or v.t.m., that is to say, "vehicles to the mile." The greater the v.t.m., the more vehicles cover a given route in a given time. There is a definite relationship between m.p.h. and v.t.m. (see Fig. 40). The most efficient average combination is approximately 25 m.p.h. with 44 v.t.m.

(c) **Routes:** The time taken for a given journey will depend largely on the width of the road to be travelled, the gradients, and the surface; also the number of available routes. The more routes there are the shorter the time taken for a large number of vehicles to travel between two given points. Where alternative routes are being used the vehicles would be split according to their estimated average speed, the faster vehicles taking the longer route, so that all should arrive at their destination together. Should there be only one available route, the most satisfactory manner is for the anticipated average speed of the slowest vehicle to be set for the journey.

Always when parking vehicles on a roadside, etc., think of cover in terms of "air." That is to say, do not place your vehicle where it could be observed by enemy aircraft. Park off road, under trees, etc. Use camouflage such as branches of trees, etc., if it is necessary to leave vehicles in exposed places. In all cases avoid bunching of vehicles, and should an obstruction be met while en route, word must be sent back quickly to the main column so that they may be deviated to avoid congestion at the obstruction.

(d) **Tactical Factor:** A column advancing is vulnerable from both air and ground. When attack is anticipated much thought must be given to choice of roads, day or night movement, speed, density, etc. Definite orders must be given to those in charge of the column as to action in the event of attack.

A density of 5 v.t.m. would scarcely be observed from the air, but a close density of say 50 v.t.m. would be very vulnerable. It is possible that in proceeding under a likelihood of attack from the air it may be necessary to advance in bounds from cover to cover.

Should attack from the air be anticipated, avoid advancing over open country such as barren plains, etc., where no cover is available. Even though the distance may be very much greater, it would be advisable under these circumstances to take the longer route through hilly country should it be available.

The enemy may create an obstruction to cause bunching. They may blow up a small bridge or fell some trees across a road, etc., that would cause the vehicles to bunch at a given spot. The vehicles could then be easily attacked from the air. Motor-cycle despatch riders should always accompany a column advancing, and should an obstruction be met the leading motor-cyclist would immediately retire and deviate the main column.

In every case where a M.T. column is advancing and attack is anticipated, particularly ground attack, a number of A.F.V.'s should advance with the column to protect them.

(B) **MOVEMENT OF MEN.**

(i.) **Loads:**

3-ton lorry	....	....	20 men.
30cwt. lorry	....	....	13 men.
15cwt. van	....	....	8 men.

One company carried in sub-section of 8 lorries (3-ton).

(ii.) **Space** occupied: **At the Halt.**

Say each lorry 7yds. long.
Space 2yds. between lorries.
Space 20yds. between blocks.

Sub-section (8 lorries) 7yds. each	....			56yds.
Gaps—7 at 2yds. between	....	....	....	14yds.

70yds.

On the Move.

(iii.) Above consists of 8 lorries (at 7yds) .... 56yds.
Assume they are moving at 25 m.p.h. and 44 v.t.m. we
get:—

> 44 vehicles 7yds. long .... 308yds.
> In a mile there are 1760yds.: subtract
> 308yds. .... 1452yds. Unoccupied.

44 vehicles divided into 1452yds. of unoccupied space
gives distance of 33yds. between the vehicles.

Therefore road space taken up by vehicles is 8 x 7yds.=
56yds.; and road space taken up by intervals is
$7 \times 33 = 231$yds. Total road space of 8 vehicles
at 25 m.p.h. at density of 44 v.t.m. is $231 + 56 =$
287yds.

(iv.) A Motor Transport column should never be dispatched
along a route beyond a point where a turning circuit
has been located from the map or, preferably, by
reconnaissance. Where there is danger of air attack or
observation, a mechanized column will not normally be
moved from its position under cover until another such
harbour has been reconnoitred to which it can proceed
immediately. During the approach march it may sometimes be necessary to select turning circuits and harbours from the map before they have been made good
by mobile troops. In these circumstances, steps will be
taken to have these locations reconnoitred as soon as
possible after they have been secured.

At any depot or temporary camp established by a
M.T. column on the move, always make sure that a
secure line of retreat is available. In other words, do
not make a base at any point where a get-away is
difficult.

(v.) **Embussing and Debussing:** Buses will be clearly marked
or numbered in chalk, and orders to units to be lifted
include the numbers of the buses which will carry them.

In a hurried move such as reinforcing a point some
miles distant with the reserve company, the company
commander will probably move ahead of the column
with a party to carry out a reconnaissance. This party

will include a transport man whose duty it is to select debussing points (close to turning circuits). Once debussed, men will move well away from the vehicles. Do not have vehicles crossing each other's paths.

4—Traffic Control.

(A)   (i.) At the starting point.
    (ii.) At all intersections.
    (iii.) Control posts 10 to 15 miles apart.
    (iv.) At destination.
    (v.) Route cards.

(B)   (i.) **At the starting point** where the column is assembled all drivers will be addressed by the officer in charge. They will be given full particulars of the journey about to be undertaken. That is to say, the destination and estimated time of arrival, route (supported by a route card if available), m.p.h. and v.tm., and full particulars relating to the trip in question.

    For mechanized columns the starting point should be well forward on the route. It is desirable for units to pass it at the given speed and density. Congestion may occur in moving from billets to the official starting point at reduced speed and increased density. Vehicles must as soon as possible accelerate to the given speed and advance at the correct density. On no account should vehicles proceed at a speed greater than that given.

    (ii.) **Route Cards:** These cards, given to drivers, include names of places en route, and times of passing same.

    (iii.) **Control Point:** An officer should be stationed at these control points and in communication with headquarters. Also he should be provided with despatch riders. He will check the time of passing, the speed, and the density.

    (iv.) **Intersections:** A traffic control man should be placed at all intersections in order to direct the column. These traffic control men will remain at their post until collected by the officer bringing up the rear.

GRAPH SHOWING RELATIONSHIP between DENSITY and MAXIMUM CRUISING SPEEDS.

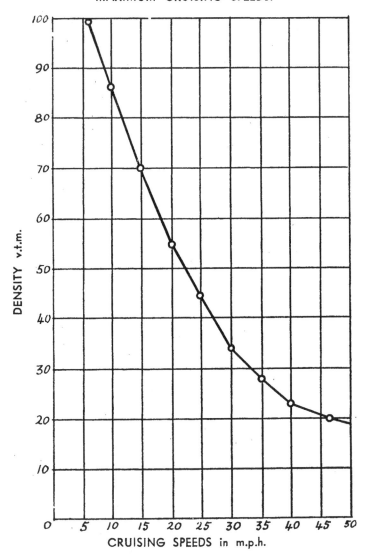

FIG. 40.

5—Speed and Density Chart.

Method of determining intervals between vehicles from the graph illustrated on Page 202 is as follows:—

If you take the bottom line and an average estimated cruising speed of 20 m.p.h., and follow this line up, it will be seen that the number of v.t.m. is 55; or if the cruising speed is 15 m.p.h. the number of v.tm. is 70.

In order to arrive at the space between the vehicles when you have a given cruising speed, refer to the chart to ascertain the number of v.t.m.

Now, if we take the average length of a truck as 7yds. and the v.t.m. as 55, trucks themselves would occupy 7 x 55 = 385yds. Therefore the space occupied by intervals is 1760—385 = 1375yds.

Now the density is 55 v.t.m. Therefore the interval between vehicles is 1375 ÷ 55 = 25yds. between vehicles.

It will be seen, therefore, that by working out this calculation in conjunction with the chart, the commander could always specify in his orders the interval in yards to be maintained between vehicles in order to attain a maximum of efficiency at the given speed.

6—Abbreviations.

M.T.	....	....	....	....	Motor Transport.
m.p.h.		....	....	....	Miles per hour.
v.t.m.		....	....	....	Vehicles to mile.
m.i.h.		....	....	....	Miles in hour (including stops).
A.F.V.		....	....	....	Armoured fighting vehicle.

7—Conclusion.

In conclusion, always remember how very important the M.T. Section of the Home Guard unit is. In times of peace there appears to be very little for the members of the M.T. Section to do. It is, therefore, most important that their interest must be maintained, and that they must be held together as an efficient and serviceable M.T. Section. Should an emergency arise it is obvious that this section would become one of great importance.

CHAPTER XII

Training.

I—Responsibility for Training. 2—Typical Syllabus. 3—Notes on Methods of Instruction. 4—Points for N.C.O.'s. 5—Advice to Young Officers and N.C.O.'s.

1—Responsibility for Training.

(i.) Every commander is responsible for the training of his unit. In the case of higher commands this implies the training of subordinate commanders on consistent lines. They in turn are responsible for the instruction and training of their own subordinates on the lines laid down by the higher command.

(ii.) The higher commands, Area, District and Dominion, will each outline the general policy for the training of their units. In each case the outline will become more detailed as it comes down the scale, for it will be possible to take into consideration more of the factors affecting local training, viz., previous training, local requirements (coastal defence, etc.), facilities (rifle ranges, etc.), equipment available, instructors available.

(iii.) Except for large scale manoeuvres the battalion is the largest training unit. In the Home Guard organization battalion training will probably not be possible, especially in country battalions, whose units are scattered. At the same time the battalion commander must draw up his syllabus, for the guidance of his company commanders. He must also concern himself with the training, both elementary and advanced, of his company officers and senior N.C.O.'s.

(iv.) The battalion commander will lay down the policy; the company commander will draw up the detailed scheme. In doing this he. must consider:—
(a) Battalion commander's policy.
(b) Time available for training.
(c) Hours for each training parade.
(d) Time taken to reach training areas.
(e) Subjects to be taught.

(f) Number of instructors.

(g) Equipment available. If there is a shortage, arrangements must be made for rotation of sections, etc.

(v.) To effect this, each commander must draw up a syllabus outlining the scope of the training his command is to be given. Subordinate commanders will then draw up their own syllabi to ensure that their formations will be efficiently trained according to the higher command syllabus.

(vi.) In the elementary stages the training unit is the section or the platoon. It is the company commander's job to see that the officers and N.C.O.'s of his company are capable and efficient, and able to train their men. The company syllabus will be drawn up to cover the battalion syllabus.

(vii.) The amount and degree of specialist training (Signals, Field Sketching, etc.) will be indicated by battalion commanders, and effect given to this by company commanders.

(viii.) Lessons in each group (drill, small arms training, fieldcraft, etc.) should be arranged in sequence and numbered. Lessons can then be referred to simply and clearly, for a parade schedule, or for record purposes. A typical battalion syllabus is given below.

(ix.) Careful records should be kept of the training each man and unit receives.

2—Typical Syllabus.

The following is a typical battalion syllabus:—

(A) Training of Men.
(B) Training of N.C.O.'s.
(C) Training of Officers.

(A) TRAINING OF MEN.

(i.) **Squad and Platoon Drill** (ref. H.G. Manual, Chap. II.)

Lesson No. 1. Squad drill: Fall in, Attention, Stand at Ease, Stand Easy.

" " 2. " " Quick March, Halt, Turns at the Halt.

" " 3. " " Turns on the March, Mark Time, Forward.

" " 4. " " Wheels, Forms, On Left Form Squad.

		5. Arms	drill:	Attention, At Ease, Stand Easy, Slope, Order.
		6.	,,	,,	Trail, Ground, Change, Present.
		7.	,,	,,	Port and Examine.
		8. Platoon drill: Fall in, Dismiss.
		9.	,,	,,	Wheel, Form, On Left Form Platoon.
		10. Field	drill:	Section deploying to arrowhead and extended line, and closing.
		11.	,,	,,	Platoon deploying.
		12. Anti-Aircraft Action.

(ii.) **Weapon Training** (ref. H.G. Manual, Chaps. III., IV., V.)

Lesson No. 1. Indication and Recognition of Targets.
     ,,   ,,   2. Fire Control.
     ,,   ,,   3. Grenades, Mills H-36.
     ,,   ,,   4. Distance Judging.
     ,,   ,,   5. The Rifle, Recognition and Parts.
     ,,   ,,   7. The Rifle, Aiming.
     ,   ,,   6. The Rifle, Loading and Unloading.
     ,,   ,,   8. The Rifle, Care and Cleaning.
     ,,   ,,   9. The Rifle, Loading Positions.
     ,,   ,,   10. The Rifle, Range Practice.
     ,,   ,,   11. Lewis Gun, Description.
     ,,   ,,   12. Lewis Gun, Stripping.
          ,,   13. Lewis Gun, Loading Gun and Magazines.
     ,,   ,,   14. Lewis Gun, Simple Stoppages.
     .   ,,   15. Lewis Gun, Holding, Aiming and Firing.

(iii.) **Fieldcraft** (ref. H.G. Manual, Chap. VI. and X.)

Lesson No. 1. Cover from View.
     ,,   ,,   2. Cover from Fire.
     ,,   ,,   3. Field Signals.
     ,,   ,,   4. Section Formations.
     ,,   ,,   5. Sentry Duties and Guards.
     ,,   ,,   6. Individual Stalks.
     ,,   ,,   7. Camouflage.
     ,,   ,,   8. Section Stalk.
     ,,   ,,   9. Movement by Night.
     ,,   ,,   10. Observation.
     ,,   ,,   11. Patrols, Reconnaissance.

,, ,, 12. Protection, Advance Guards.
,, ,, 13. Patrols, Fighting.
,, ,, 14. Patrols, Standing.
,, ,, 15. The Attack.
,, ,, 16. Protection, Flank and Rear Guards.
,, ,, 17. Defence Works.
,, ,, 18. The Defence.
,, ,, 19. Withdrawal.

(B) TRAINING OF N.C.O.'s.

(i.) Training as for men.
(ii.) Methods of Instruction, Mutual.
(iii.) Elementary Map-reading.
(iv.) Patrols, Day and Night.
(v.) Orders, Messages and Reports.
(vi.) Section and Platoon in Attack.
(vii.) Section and Platoon in Defence.
(viii.) Field Obstacles and Defensive Works.
(ix.) Street Fighting.
(x.) Withdrawal.
(xi.) Sanitation.

(C) TRAINING OF OFFICERS.

(i.) Training as for N.C.O.'s, but to a more advanced stage.
(ii.) Co-operation with other arms.
(iii.) Improvised weapons.
(iv.) Map-reading and Reconnaissance.
(v.) Tactics.

(D) The company commander will set out fuller details for each of the above lessons, and the platoon commanders will see that their N.C.O.'s know exactly what is required for each lesson they have to give a day or two before the training parade. The programme of training should as a rule be drawn up a week ahead, so that all instructors have adequate time for preparation of their lessons.

3—Notes on Methods of Instruction.

(A) The requirements for a good instructor are:—
(i.) He must know thoroughly the matter he is teaching.
(ii.) His demonstrations must be well executed. There must

be nothing indecisive or careless in his own bearing and movements.

(iii.) He must have confidence in himself and in his ability to teach and control his men.

(iv.) He must be able to explain his points clearly and con-cisely, without repeating the drill-book words parrot-fashion.

(v.) He must be tactful but firm; ready to answer relevant questions from the squad, but able to suppress frivolous questions.

(vi.) He must be keen and efficient, to arouse keenness and efficiency in his men.

(B) In teaching any matter the plan should be PEDIER:—

(i.) Preparation.
(ii.) Explanation.
(iii.) Demonstration.
(iv.) Interrogation.
(v.) Execution.
(vi.) Repetition.

(i.) All lessons must be prepared beforehand and the neces-sary gear put ready to hand. The scope of the lessons, the sequence and the points to be stressed should be worked out or revised.

(iii.) Explanation should be brief and to the point. Demon-stration can often replace tedious talking. For both explanation and demonstration make sure the squad can see and hear. A semi-circle is a suitable arrangement. Let the squad stand easy, or sit down, whenever pos-sible. A tired or uncomfortable squad are not easy to keep interested.

(iii.) Demonstration must be as nearly perfect as the instructor can make it. A movement carried out by a succession of movements should be demonstrated first as the complete movement, and then each stage should be taken separately and demonstrated. In rifle move-ments, for instance, each move is shown separately, and the squad imitate and practise the moves separately until they are ready to put them together.

(iv.) To make sure that the squad understand the details of the lesson, the instructor will go over the ground by questioning individual men on separate points. It is a valuable check on his own instructing to know what points he has failed to make clear.

(v.) Execution, as indicated above, may often usefully be combined with demonstration; but nothing should be attempted by the squad until the instructor is sure they can do it with some success. Mistakes made in the early stages are often hard to eradicate.

(vi.) Repetition is the key to real proficiency. A man or a squad can be brought by training to a high standard of performance; but unless regular practice is given, proficiency soon drops. Be careful not to overdo practice and so make the work dull.

(C) (i.) A squad who understand the purpose of each portion of their training, and who are given opportunities for discussion with their instructors, will learn more readily and more intelligently than those whose training is mere routine.

(ii.) During any training period vigorous lessons should alternate with easier ones. Strenuous physical work or inactivity during lectures equally impair efficiency if too prolonged. The early part of the day is the best for the active work, late in the day for the lighter.

(iii.) For instruction men are best grouped on the basis of their knowledge or experience. Unneeded instruction leads to loss of enthusiasm.

(iv.) Work already done will be most efficiently practised if it is given even a slight new turn or variation.

(v.) For most elementary instruction a squad of eight to twelve men is the ideal.

4—Points for N.C.O.'s.

(A) **LEADERSHIP.**

(i.) A leader must have the confidence of his men, and to gain this he must have confidence in himself. He must be able to make up his mind, and having done so, to stick to his decision. He must keep calm. To show doubt or indecision is a sure way of shaking the confidence of his men. A stout-hearted man will always go on trying, and by doing so he will instil his own fighting spirit into his men.

(ii.) Loyalty is an essential of leadership: unless a leader is himself loyal to his superiors, he cannot expect loyal support from his subordinates.

(iii.) He must understand discipline: he must command his section firmly, but with common sense and fairness. He must give orders clearly, and having given an order, he must insist on its being efficiently carried out.

(iv.) A section leader must know:
(a) The organization of his battalion.
(b) His responsibility for training his section.
(c) His duties in the field.
(d) How his section acts as part of the platoon.

(v.) He should encourage **esprit de corps** in his section that leads to friendly rivalry within the platoon. He must make each man realize that he is relied on by others: that one man can let the section down in training as well as in the field.

(B) MAN MANAGEMENT.

(i.) A section leader must supervise the personal cleanliness and the sanitary arrangements of his section (see Appendix on Hygiene).

(ii.) He must be absolutely fair, and avoid victimizing an unsatisfactory man. Fatigues should be equally distributed. Some men are quick to find a way of avoiding arduous or unpleasant duties: others will undertake cheerfully any task they are ordered to do. A section commander must study his men, learn their characteristics, and then handle them accordingly.

(iii.) Men should be encouraged to bring reasonable complaints to their section commander. Imaginary wrongs brooded over, or talked over among the section, soon become magnified. There is nothing that cannot be put right if a reasonable approach to authority is made; and many imagined causes for complaint originate in misunderstandings.

(iv.) A good N.C.O. after a tiring day, or in unpleasant conditions, will make certain of his men's comfort before seeking his own. Men quickly notice and appreciate an N.C.O. who is doing his job unselfishly.

5—Advice to Young Officers and N.C.O.'s.

(i.) It is the duty of officers and N.C.O.'s to set a very high standard and example of loyalty, behaviour and turn-out. They must be firm but fair, efficient but not officious.

(ii.) They must look after the interests of their men, and while letting nothing go, be prepared to help the lame ducks.

(iii.) When receiving an order they must make absolutely certain they understand exactly what to do. They must check the order over in their minds, and if in doubt about anything, ask questions to get it clear. If they fail to check up, one day they will go away and find that they do not understand the order, when it is too late to check up. This may lead to disaster not only for themselves but for others. In short, they must make certain of what is required before saying "Very good, sir."

(iv.) When giving an order, they must give it in such a fashion that there is no manner of doubt in the mind of the recipient that the order is intended for him, and that what is required is understood. They must not, for example, say, "Some of you do so-and-so," but "No. 1 Section," or "Smith, Lewis and Macdonald."

(v.) Every officer and N.C.O. must remember that in war the lives of his men will often depend on his knowledge of his job, and his efficiency and his ability to command. It is his duty to do his utmost to make himself fit for the job.

(vi.) Since men of all ages and ranks are enlisted in the Home Guard, young instructors must always remember that although their own knowledge of drill and field training is up to date, they have not been tried out under fire, whereas many of those they may be instructing have had actual experience "In the Field." They should, therefore, be always ready to accept advice from men with such service. What is wanted in the Home Guard is the spirit of comradeship and willing co-operation which is found on the field of battle.

APPENDIX 1.

Hygiene and Sanitation.

1. GENERAL.

A high standard of health is a sign of efficiency. To achieve this requires the co-operation of all ranks.

Every commander is responsible for the health of his command, and for applying all the necessary measures to ensure it. He is also responsible for the sanitary condition of the area occupied by his command, irrespective of the period for which it is occupied. Each unit will do well to have men specially trained as sanitary police to supervise all sanitary work; but all officers and N.C.O.'s must know the principles of sanitation.

2. PERSONAL CLEANLINESS.

This is of the utmost importance. Provision must be made for regular baths or bathing facilities. Underclothing should be washed regularly, and outer clothing disinfected if necessary at least once a week.

A sharp watch must be kept for skin affections such as impetigo and for the appearance of lice. Any skin outbreak must be reported for medical treatment. If an outbreak occurs those affected should be segregated for washing purposes. Towels are a regular source of contagion.

Teeth must be regularly brushed. In the absence of toothpaste common salt will serve as a substitute.

The indiscriminate use of eating and drinking utensils should be forbidden.

After marches, etc., feet should be washed, and then inspected by platoon commanders. Blisters should be promptly treated with iodine and foot-powder. If fresh socks are not available, the dirty ones should be changed to the opposite feet.

3. CAMPS.

To maintain a high standard of health, flies must not be allowed to breed. This implies careful provision for the disposal of all waste, excreta, etc., and strict supervision of their disposal.

212

(i.) **Latrines and Urinals** will be made immediately on arrival in camp or bivouac, and the sites marked with an L in stones when the unit leaves. They should be placed as far as possible from the cookhouses, and to leeward of the camp site. In no case will open trench latrines be used where it is possible to construct either deep trench or bucket latrines.

(a) Deep trench latrines should be sited where there is no possibility of contaminating water supplies. They are dug 6ft. to 8ft. deep, with the back wall of the trench sloping outwards from the top. They are provided with boxed-in seats and automatically closing lids. The number of seats should be approximately five per cent. of the number of men. They are to be filled in when their contents come to within two feet of the ground level.

(b) Bucket latrines must have flyproof covers to all receptacles, boxed-in seats with automatically closing lids wherever possible. Three inches of cresol solution ($1\frac{1}{2}$oz. to 1gal.) should be put in each bucket. The contents must be removed and buried, and the receptacles cleansed and wiped with heavy oil every day.

(c) Shallow trench latrines should be 3ft. long, 2ft. wide, and 1ft. deep.

The best type of field urinal for day and night use is made of plain galvanized iron: it is in the form of a trough with a high back and a pipe leading from the lower end of the trough to a soak pit. The soak pit is made by digging a hole up to 4ft. deep and filling it with rubble or shingle. This is covered, a foot below the surface, with sacking, on top of which is put sand. The turf from the top of the hole is best replaced.

The inside of all tins used for urinals should be painted daily with a thin coating of heavy oil. The outsides will be whitewashed so as to be more visible at night.

Urinating indiscriminately in camp or bivouac areas must be strictly prohibited.

(ii.) **Cookhouses:** Floors should have the top 6in. dug up, treated with heavy oil, and rammed down well.

All foodstuffs must be protected from contamination by flies. Dishcloths are to be boiled every evening and hung up to dry. No unbaked sand or mud must be used for cleaning knives or utensils. Washing up must be done on a table, not on the ground, and a soak pit with grease trap is essential.

An improvised grease trap, suitable for a halt of short duration, is made by filtering the slop water into a soak pit through brushwood or straw which is subsequently burnt.

Nothing unconnected with the preparation of food is permitted in any cookhouse. Meat safes are to be kept clean, and in the shade.

The cleanliness of the cooks, and of their clothing, is of the highest importance. They must keep their hands, mouths, teeth scrupulously clean. No cook suffering from a cold or any other disease, or with ulcerated gums or mouth, should be allowed to remain on duty. The cleanliness of cookhouse fatigue parties must also be carefully supervised.

(iii.) **Refuse** will be disposed of by burning whenever possible. Carcases of animals will be disembowelled, the internal organs buried, and the rest burnt. Refuse that cannot be burnt will be buried. It must never be left in open pits. A thick layer of earth must be put over each layer of refuse as it is emptied into the pit.

(iv.) **Drinking Water:** All water receptacles, from tanks to water-bottles, must be emptied and thoroughly cleaned once a week, after which they are to be disinfected before refilling. The disinfecting is carried out by swilling with water to which twice the amount of water-sterilizing powder needed for drinking water sterilization has been added.

APPENDIX 2.

Tank Hunting and Destruction.

1. Tanks are big, and strong and bullying in their use, and like most bullies, have some very vulnerable points. Trained tank-hunters, chosen for their courage, coolness and readiness to carry the fight to the enemy, can become such a pest and potential danger to tanks and their crews that the value of both as fighting units can be reduced by more than half.

2. TASK.

To harry, molest, surprise, worry and otherwise terrorise enemy tank crews so that they soon become convinced that their tanks are traps in which they will sooner or later be caught and destroyed. Tank-hunters must immediately take the initiative and search for tanks to destroy. Do not be passive. Ambush, snipe and trick enemy tank crews until you have destroyed **every** tank in your area. Once a tank is found it must become a point of honour not to let it escape you.

3. PERSONNEL.

As already stated, tank-hunters will be selected for training on account of their bravery, cool-headedness, and ability to make a marauding tank their quarry.

4. EQUIPMENT.

Equipment for hunters will be simple. Sections should be as mobile as possible. Motor-cycles are the best form of transport. In addition to the anti-tank rifle, L.G.M. and rifles, some of the following will be useful according to the tasks in hand:—

Hand grenades (either issue or home-made).
Petrol bombs (Molotov Cocktails).
Smoke candles or bombs.
Anti-tank mines.
Axes and saws.
Explosives and demolitions.
Crowbars (for breaking tank tracks).
Shotguns (for firing into drivers' and gunners' slits).

5. TRAINING.

Men must be trained to be quick-witted and confident. They must be bold and swift-moving. High morale and determination are most essential. Men must be physically fit and "spoiling" for a fight with enemy tanks. Fieldcraft must be understood thoroughly. Night work is an important factor. Sections should be trained constantly in "attacks," "hunts," "movements with equipment" in darkness. Map-reading will also be taught and a high standard is required. Men should be shown how to construct an ambush and then made to make their own, avoiding stereotyped design or construction. Thus everyone is encouraged to use his own ideas. Men will have a thorough and complete knowledge of all the weapons previously mentioned. Petrol bombs must not be thrown, but "lobbed" on to the tops of tanks. This gives a better result, as the burning mixture runs down all round and has a much greater effect. All men should be able to drive.

6. TACTICAL ACTION OF TANK-HUNTERS.

They will be given an area to be responsible for, with a roving commission in that area. An area known to them will be selected if possible. They should be mobile, ..e., motor-cyclists, etc.

Information is necessary, but it has been found that descriptions by untrained folk are generally very distorted when dealing with tanks seen, so hunters will need to be able to gauge accurately the true story.

Sites for ambushes will be reconnoitred, and if necessary the materials for constructing the ambush will be stored nearby. The basis of the plan will be to place a block, or ambush, in such a position that the enemy will come on it unexpectedly and with no room to manoeuvre, will be at the mercy of the hunters. A defile is the best illustration. As soon as the leading tank or A.F.V. has stopped at the ambush, the retreat of the column is blocked, and the hunters then set to work, making sure that **every** tank or A.F.V. is destroyed or put out of commission.

Booby traps can be used very effectively. Wire stretched across a road at a height of about 3ft. will do for motor-cyclists acting as "eyes" for tanks. Anything will do as long as it will cause the tank or A.F.V. to stop and present a better target for the bombs or other offensive weapons of the hunters. A row of innocuous soup plates upended across a paddock or street will cause the driver of a tank to stop and investigate the possibility of their being a land mine. A few blankets strung across a street as though hiding a tank trap or mine-field will serve as well. If you can slow up the enemy's action you are doing a good job.

During daylight hunters will search out most likely spots for tanks to hide at night, when their use is very restricted. At night tank-hunters have the advantage, and for that reason must be experts at night moving and finding direction, etc. (see chapters on Fieldcraft). Stalk the tanks with every weapon you can use—grenades, incendiary bombs by day; bayonets etc., when resting or at night. As soon as you have destroyed one tank, immediately start looking for another.

Try to make each sortie with a different offensive weapon, or at least by using a different method. Avoid being stereo-typed. Every man in a tank-hunting section will have at least a dozen good ideas. Use them all.

7. ENEMY TANKS.

The modern tank has many disadvantages, each of which will be exploited to the full by the trained tank-hunter.

(a) **Blindness:** There are only the slits for the driver, the gunner and the commander, and at no time is more than 10 per cent. of the surrounding country visible from inside the tank. Likewise, at ground level, nothing within a radius of 15ft. can be seen. Therefore, if you are lying on the ground **within** 15ft. of a tank you are out of sight. This is just the ideal distance for lobbing your death-dealing "cocktail."

(b) **Field of Fire:** The guns cannot hit anything within a radius of 20ft. of the tank or fire above an angle of 25 degrees. Therefore, if you are on a high bank or at a second-storey window, you might be seen but the enemy would be unable to fire on you. On the other hand, you would be in an ideal position to drop your bombs on to the roof of the tank. A tank could not fire into a deep "slit-trench," and as the turrets revolve very slowly, a simultaneous attack from various directions will be bound to have the required result.

(c) **Tracks:** Without its tracks the tank is useless. Ramming a crowbar or heavy wooden batten in between the track and the driving sprocket will wrench off or break the track. Eight sticks of gelignite and a detonator if run over will destroy the track on any known tank.

(d) **Crews:** Moving at speed over comparatively short distances is very tiring, and crews constantly threatened by trained hunters soon realise that their task is fairly hopeless.

(e) **Petrol:** Tanks must have petrol, and if the sources of supply are destroyed the tanks are effectively combated.

8. CAPTURED TANKS.

Should you capture a tank by killing its crew, it should be handed at once to the experts for examination. If there is the slightest likelihood of it falling into the hands of the enemy again, however, it should be destroyed at once. Some methods of destruction:—

(a) Petrol bombs dropped inside.

(b) Breaking or removing tracks is effective until spare parts can be brought up.

(c) Breaking driver's controls (including gear lever), water jacket of engine (with sledge hammer), carburettor or fuel pump, sprockets (blown off with gelignite).

9. KEEPING TOUCH.

If you come across a detachment which is too large to attack, then stalk it so it cannot get away from you, and send a message back with full details of enemy's direction, strength (do not exaggerate), method of advance, and all other points which will be useful.

10. ANTI-TANK MINES.

These play the same part against tanks as wire does against infantry, and unless they are kept under defensive fire they will be useless. On discovering anti-tank mines, tanks will try to detour round them, drive off the covering troops, and then remove the balance of the mines. This can be avoided if the mines are placed so that they are encountered unexpectedly and deviation is awkward. Close spacing should be used.

11. TANK OBSTACLES (General).

Tank traps will be built as explained in Field Engineering, but the following are a few guiding rules:—

(a) A tank cannot cross a gap that is slightly over half the tank's length unless it approaches at high speed, when it might be able to jump.

(b) A tank cannot climb a vertical face which is over the height of the track where it passes over the "idler" wheel or leading sprocket. In case of trenches or banks of earth, use a 5ft. minimum.

(c) A tank is unlikely to surmount an obstacle which causes the floor level of the tank to rise, from the forward end, to an angle of more than 45 degrees with the horizontal.

(d) Stumps will stop tanks by raising the tracks off the ground by fouling the belly of the tank between the tracks. For this purpose use stumps not less than 12in. in diameter or not less than 2ft. 3in. in height.

12. TYPICAL TANK AMBUSH.

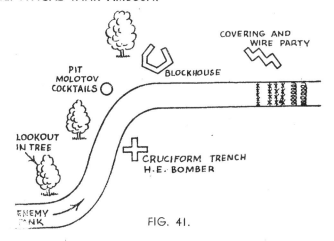

FIG. 41.

The enemy tank is enticed by the blockhouse to slow down and attack. As soon as it reduces speed it is assaulted on two sides from the trench and pit.

A section of nine men is sufficient to operate an ambush:

One man as look-out, one H.E. bomber in the trench, one man with Molotov Cocktails in the pit, three men in the blockhouse and three men operating and covering the wire barricade.

The look-out gives a visual signal to the blockhouse, and the blockhouse warns the rest of the party. When the tank is within 100yds. the blockhouse opens fire, not primarily to do damage, but to attract the tank's attention. Should the tank slow down to attack, it is itself attacked from the pit and trench. If several tanks are expected, similar parties should operate at intervals of 75 to 100yds. along the road.

The look-out and the blockhouse party stand by with rifles waiting for the tank crew to be forced into the open.

IMPORTANT.

These are very general rules for the guidance of tank-hunting sections and platoons, but as these hunters are chosen for their initiative and ability to move to the offensive, no doubt they will very soon have a thousand and one nasty little surprises awaiting the arrival of an unwary tank crew. If you come across ten tanks and only "out" nine of them, you've failed in your mission.

APPENDIX 3.

Sand Table.

1. **GENERAL.**

For indoor training in tactics either a blackboard or a sand table can be used. The conditions and situations can be more clearly pictured on a sand table, and the exercises are more interesting, and thus the more valuable.

2. **EQUIPMENT.**

(a) A tray approximately 6ft. by 3ft. 6in., with sides 6in. high. This can be placed on a table or across two forms.

(b) Sufficient sand to fill the tray about two-thirds full.

(c) Model trees, bushes, etc., made with wire and green wool.

(d) Model houses, sheds, gates, etc., made from small blocks of wood and painted suitable colours.

(e). Strips of sponge or loofah coloured green and brown to represent hedges.

(f) A quantity of coloured sawdust. Sawdust can easily be dyed by placing it in a bag and immersing it in the dye solution.

3. **CONSTRUCTION OF LANDSCAPES.**

(a) Mould the sand to represent the conformation of the ground as required for the exercise.

(b) Put in roads and tracks with sawdust, light-coloured powder or tapes.

(c) Add fields and colour, using natural coloured sawdust for corn, green for grassland, dark-brown for ploughed land, and mixture of brown and green for open heath.

(d) Put in houses, trees and other details.

(e) Divide the sides of the sand table with chalk marks representing divisions of 100 yards according to the scale.

(f) Write the names of the various places on slips of paper and put them on the sand table.

4. **SAND TABLE EXERCISES.**

(a) Early exercises should be simple, each one dealing with one or two considerations only. As the class gains experience the exercises can be made more complicated. The object of the lessons is not to get stereotyped solutions to every problem, but to get the class to realize the factors involved in making a decision and practice in weighing those factors up.

(b) The preparation of an exercise by the instructor involves:—

(i.) A lecture on the subject of the exercise. Chapters VI. Fieldcraft, VIII. Engineering, and X. Tactics will provide all the material required.

(ii.) A narrative of the events leading up to the situation represented on the sand table, which is the subject for the problems.

(iii.) A series of problems, one following on another as the situation is pictured developing.

(iv.) A plan of the sand table model to be used for the exercise.

(c) The exercises should be conducted in the following manner:

(i.) Study the sand table, pointing out names of places, north point, scale, etc.

(ii.) Read out the narrative for the exercise, and explain it to the class.

(iii.) Take a series of problems arising from the situation outlined, dealing with one problem before mentioning the next. Let the class consider what action should be taken.

(iv.) Call on class in turn to give their solutions. In cases where fire orders, etc., have to be given, the N.C.O. giving the solution should give his orders to the rest of the class as he would to his section in the field.

(v.) Sum up the solutions, discuss them, and give your own well-considered solution as the best, but not necessarily the only, course of action to meet the situation.

5. **NOTES.**

(a) Don't use the same model too often, even though many problems can be set on a single model: the class soon become tired of it.

(b) Make the models as bright and realistic as possible, but not too elaborate. It should be possible to set up a new model in under an hour.

(c) Sections and men should be represented by pegs, etc., and these should be moved by the N.C.O.'s as the exercise proceeds.

6. A TYPICAL EXERCISE—Use of Ground: A Section Stalk.

(A) **Object of Exercise:** To train the section commander in the use of ground and of section formation.

(B) **Introduction:**

(i.) "Infantry Training" reads: "The aims of the platoon and section commander should be to advance as close as possible to the enemy position without undue loss and without having to check the speed of the attack by opening fire."

(ii.) To put this into effect the section commander must be trained to:—

(a) First select the position of observation from which the line can be observed.

(b) Select the position from which fire is to be opened.

(c) Pick the line that is the best covered.

(d) Consider the obstacles to be crossed.

(e) Protection.

(f) Maintain direction. Prominent objects on the line should be picked, and pointed out to the whole section.

(g) Adopt the formation which best conforms to the ground over which he is moving (see Fieldcraft, Chapter VI., Section 5c).

(C) **The Exercise.**

(i.) **Narrative:** An enemy patrol has been located at WHITE FARM. You are O.C. No. 3 Section, and you are in position just in rear of GREEN WOOD.

(ii.) **Problem:** By the use of ground, to lead your section so close to the enemy patrol that you can shoot with a certainty of killing them.

(iii.) **Method of Conducting Exercise:**

(a) Having given out the narrative and the problem to the class, show them No. 3 Section, which you have placed at X.

(b) The class considers the problem.

(c) Then in turn ask them the questions:—

Q. I: How near do you think you should get to be able to shoot with the certainty of killing them?

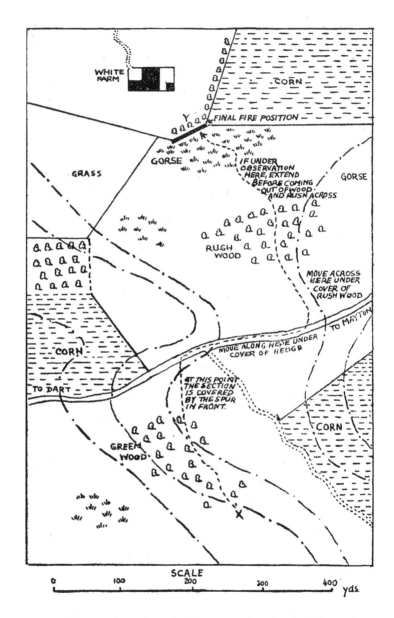

FIG. 42—Plan of sand-table set up for the typical exercise.

Q. 2: What position would you select to observe your line of approach?

Q. 3: What position would you choose as your final fire position, and why?

Q. 4: What line gives you the best covered approach?

Q. 5: What obstacles are in your way?

Q. 6: Move your section on the sand table along the line you have selected.

(D) NOTES FOR SOLUTION.

A. 1: Not more than 100 yards away, nearer if possible. (Bring out the point that, whereas on the range under ideal conditions men may be able to shoot accurately up to 500 yards, it is a very different matter when (a) they have just done a possibly fatiguing movement, (b) they are naturally excited.)

A. 2: The high ground at X.

A. 3: The hedge at Y, because—

(a) It is near the objective.

(b) It appears to be a good position.

(c) It has the best line of approach.

A. 4: A suggested line is shown on the map by a dotted line. This line makes the most use of natural cover.

A. 5: The only obstacles in this case are the open spaces that have to be crossed between the covered areas.

A. 6: This will bring out the use of the various formations. The section commander must be able to split his advance up into "bounds," and say what formation he would adopt for the various "bounds."

APPENDIX 4.

Appreciations and Orders.

(A) **APPRECIATION OF THE SITUATION:** Before making his plan, a commander must consider all factors that are likely to have an effect on the operation. It is useless just to make a plan without taking into consideration the strength of the enemy, the nature of the ground, what the enemy is likely to do, etc. Rational thinking is essential, and an Appreciation is a review of the situation through a series of logical deductions up to the final paragraph, which consists of the definite details of the plan. The following are the general headings of an appreciation:—

Appreciation of the Situation from the Point of View of the Commander "A" Coy. 1st Bn. XX Home Guard.

Map. Ref., e.g., Hawke's Bay Sheet N. 124 ....Time
1 in. = 1 mile   ....Date
                                                    ....Place

(i.) **The Object,** e.g.: "To defend the area............................
against an enemy landing, etc."

(ii.) **Considerations Affecting the Attainment of the Object:**
(a) Strength of opposing forces—Personnel.
                                            Weapons.

(b) Topography: consider how the following will affect movements of enemy and own troops:—
> **Woods.**
> Hills.
> Rivers.
> Beaches.
> Defiles.
> Bridges.
> Vulnerable points.

(c) Consider how intercommunication may be maintained by:—
> Signaller.
> Runner.
> Cyclist.
> Telephone.
> Wireless.

(d) Weather. Note particularly time of sunrise and sunset. Note how rain affects roads and country.

(e) Time and space. Consider time available and time required to cover distances in relation to rate of movement.

(iii.) **Courses:**

(a) **Open to Enemy:** Put yourself in the enemy's position and consider plans which would be likely to gain his objective. Give short reasons for each suggested course, and do not suggest a course that is tactically unsound.

(b) **Open to Our Side:** From the above discuss all courses that are open to our side, giving reasons for and against each. From these decide on one course and make a plan.

(iv.) **The Plan:** This must be clear and definite, and in sufficient detail so that orders can be written from it.

(B) **ORDERS:** Orders are given either verbally or in writing. They should be given out in the following logical sequence so that the person giving the order may ensure that nothing is omitted, and at the same time the recipient, being used to this sequence, can grasp the details with a minimum of delay.

(i.) **Information:**

(a) **Regarding the Enemy:** Only give information likely to help recipients to carry out their tasks.

(b) **Regarding Our Own Troops:** As for (a). Also necessary information as to what other troops are doing.

(ii.) **Intention:** State briefly what you intend to do with your men, e.g., "We will attack enemy and drive him from his located position at X."

(iii.) **Method:** Describe clearly how you are going to carry out your intention. Points usually included in this paragraph will be found in Chapter X.

(iv.) **Administration:** Any alteration in normal equipment, location of platoon truck, supply of ammunition, medical arrangements, tools, etc.

(v.) **Intercommunication:** Position of company or platoon headquarters, light signals, runners, communication with aircraft, etc.

ADDENDA

1. COMPANY DRILL.

C (vii.) **"AT THE HALT, FORM CLOSE COLUMN OF PLATOONS."** No. I Platoon commander gives the command, "No. I PLATOON, AT THE HALT, ON THE LEFT, FORM—PLATOON." Similarly the other platoon commanders as close column distance from the platoon in front is reached.

2. BOMBING DRILL (with dummy grenades).

Stand facing target, with grenade on the ground.

"ONE"—Take up grenade in the right hand, base of the fingers round the lever, and hold it slightly forward of and above the right hip, hooking the left forefinger through the ring.

"TWO"—Turn right, carrying right foot back.

"THREE"—Holding the left hand still, take the right arm sharply back. Glance down to see that the whole of the pin has been removed. Drop the right knee, and raise the left arm in the direction of the target.

"FOUR"—Throw the grenade, with right still straight, straightening the right knee, and swinging the body as well as the arm.

HINTS AND MAXIMS FOR HOME GUARDS

Always inspect your rifle after use, to make certain it is not loaded. This is done by 'easing-springs', i.e., releasing the bolt and working it back and forth several times, making certain that your finger is away from the trigger. At the immediate rear of the trigger-guard there is a small release trigger. If this is pressed the magazine itself can be withdrawn.

Never in any circumstances point the rifle in the direction of your comrades, either when loading or unloading, or even when you are carrying it.

When about to engage the enemy always carry the rifle loaded, but with the safety catch on, so that when you open up the engagement from cover, as suggested, no noise – as from operating the bolt – will reveal your presence before you fire.

Always keep your rifle clean. After firing clean the barrel by taking out the bolt and drawing the 'pull-through' through the barrel. An oil-bottle and 'pull-through' are to be found in the aperture in the butt, the brass cover of which can be raised by inserting a coin or knife-blade in the nitch for that purpose.

Never carry the rifle at ease in the shoulder when patrolling or operating. Even at night and in complete darkness, bolts, heel-plates and the tabs of the rifle-sling, etc., show distinctly. Always carry the rifle on the side that is in shadow, and carry it down the side in the manner of 'secure arms', taking care that the heel-plate of the butt is snugged under the armpit, and is not visible.

The barrel of the rifle should be cleaned out regularly with hot water. This is best done by removing the bolt, opening the cut-out, and inserting a funnel in the breech of the barrel. Care must be taken to ensure that the water is boiling, not warm, and the rifle must be dried out thoroughly afterwards and carefully oiled through. Your rifle is your best friend, treat it so and it will never let you down.

An excerpt from the 'Press' – 'The soldier was slinging his rifle over his shoulder when it went off, to the consternation of people in the public-bar; a bullet went through one of the windows. The people later were inclined to treat the matter as a joke. The soldiers left the bar thinking the only damage done was a small 'hole' in the plate glass.

Unfortunately, however, a trolley bus was passing at the time and a man who was riding on the upper deck was injured in the left eye.'

This emphasises how necessary it is for the Home Guard always to see that his rifle is empty when not in action. It is the practice in the armed forces to have always an arms inspection after a parade or patrol, when all arms are 'ported' for inspection by an officer. If for some reason this has been omitted, 'case-springs' yourself in the manner detailed at the commencement of these hints. It is a very simple matter, but it does save the danger of episodes like the one mentioned above.

To attack the enemy parachute-trooper while still in the air, do not follow him with the rifle as he drops but, taking aim a little lower in the direction he is dropping, remain with finger at first-pressure on the trigger, let him glide down into the sights, then fire. The chances of missing are greatly minimized by this method.

There are two prime maxims in connection with firing for the Home Guard to remember. First, the shorter the range the more accurate the fire. Second, the best result is obtained from fire which is combined with surprise.

Remember the blade of the foresight on the service rifle entirely covers a standing man at 600 yards; kneeling at 300 yards; and lying-low at 200 yards.

In normal atmosphere all parts of a man are distinctly visible at 200 yards. At 300 yards the features are indistinct. At 400 yards the body outline appears normal, but the features are not seen at all.

To move quietly when on patrol, lift the feet clear of the ground in the manner of marking-time, replacing the feet flatly on the ground (i.e., the heel and toe meeting the ground at the same time). Each foot should be replaced on the ground before advancing the other leg.

If there is any light in the vicinity of the patrol at night, either flares, searchlights or a bright horizon, always move with your face and hands in shadow, never raise your face or look up without shielding it. It can be seen, even in a bad light, for quite a distance.

When enemy is in the vicinity, leaders of sections should halt after every six or eight paces, making sufficient pause to be able to ascertain any possible indication that there are enemy in the immediate neighbourhood.

If you are wearing a steel helmet when passing through woods with enemy in the vicinity, remove it and carry it on your arm. The noise of low hanging branches striking it can be heard from quite a distance and will possibly reveal your presence to an enemy.

When patrolling through woods likely to contain enemy, the danger from noise of unexpected collision with unseen obstacles at night can be minimized if the free hand is extended to full length before one, and if each foot is replaced firmly before moving the other. Always walk in a broken step when on patrol, a measured step can be heard a long distance away.

To ascertain better the whereabouts of an enemy at night, do not stand still and look around. Drop down on one knee. From this lower position he will be clearly seen in silhouette.

It is useful to remember that on hard ground a knife-blade inserted in the earth to its full extent will, if the ear is placed to the handle, record the footsteps of persons approaching up to quite an appreciable distance. In wet or boggy country, squelching reveals itself for an almost similar distance.

On moonlight nights always move from shadow to shadow, and keep well down inside any available undulations in the ground. If surprised lie still on the ground, it is quite impossible for the enemy to locate you without considerable searching. Never on any occasion move along the sky-line.

Never, fire on a lone enemy, it might disclose your position to a much larger force with tragic results. If a lone enemy approaches, remain concealed until he has passed, then overpower him or dispatch him, without noise. If you are acting as scout, contact your pivot, who in turn will warn the section, then let him right past you for the section to deal with. Never separate sufficiently to become detached from your party.

If you are engaging an enemy parachute-trooper and there is no cover available, lie prone on the ground and fire from this position. You present less of yourself as a target and consequently are less likely to get hit.

If during an engagement with enemy troopers you become inadvertently separated from your section and are in danger of discovery, lie down in cover if it is available. It is much safer to do this than attempt to return to your section and so give away their position. You can do so later, particularly if a pre-arranged rendezvous has been selected by the section leader.

If you have the misfortune to become a casualty, do not panic. Always try to stop the bleeding. This can sometimes be done by placing a pad made from a handkerchief over the wound and applying a steady pressure of the fingers over the site of the wound. If this fails to stop the bleeding take a piece of bandage, or even the braces strap, wrap it tightly round the limb above the wound, knot it, then insert a piece of stick or pencil and twist it round several times to tighten the bandage, then secure the stick by another bandage or cord to prevent it unwinding. This tourniquet should not be left tightened for more than fifteen minutes at a stretch, as it is liable to stop the blood from flowing again. It can, however, be left in position and re-tightened again should bleeding resume.

To avoid collision on patrol at night the section should proceed in single file with approximately three or four paces between each man. When the leader halts the remainder do so instantly.

All equipment should be examined before going on patrol, to ensure that it is free from anything loose and likely to rattle or make a noise. Care should be taken to refrain from talking, coughing, or even whispering. Signal to one another or make some sign, or if it is absolutely necessary to hold conversation, do so in the veriest whisper.

Make certain that the steel helmets do not come in contact with one another.

If a noise is inadvertently made, stand quite still, never attempt to retreat hastily; pause awhile, then slowly lower yourself to the ground and 'snake' your way backwards out of danger.